The Way of
Wisdom
in Pastoral
Counseling

The Way of *Wisdom*
in **Pastoral Counseling**

Daniel S. Schipani

Institute of Mennonite Studies
2003

Published by Institute of Mennonite Studies, 3003 Benham Avenue, Elkhart IN 47517-1999, U.S.A. (www.ambs.edu/IMS)

Printed in the United States of America by Evangel Press, Nappanee, Indiana

ISBN 0-936273-34-8

Library of Congress Cataloging-in-Publication Data

The way of wisdom in pastoral counseling / Daniel S. Schipani
      p. cm.
Includes bibliographical references (p.   ).
  ISBN 0-936273-34-8
  1. Pastoral counseling. 2. Wisdom–Religious aspects–Christianity.
I. Title.
  BV4012.2.S32 2003
  253.5–dc21
                        2003010762

Cover design by Mary E. Klassen

Contents

Gratitudes   vii

Introduction   1
PASTORAL COUNSELING IN CONTEXT   2
THE REASON FOR THIS BOOK   3
THESIS AND SCOPE   7
FINAL WORDS   10

1 | Reflecting on the practice   11
FOUR WINDOWS TO PASTORAL COUNSELING   11
AN EMERGING VISION FOR PASTORAL COUNSELING   26

2 | Reclaiming wisdom as the heart   37
THE REIGN OF GOD AND WISDOM IN THE LIGHT OF GOD   37
WISDOM IN THE BIBLICAL TRADITION   40
JESUS AND THE WISDOM OF GOD   46
INTERLUDE: UNDERSTANDING AND APPROPRIATING WISDOM   52
WISDOM AND PASTORAL COUNSELING   55

3 | Reframing pastoral counseling   65
VIEWED AND PRACTICED PASTORALLY   68
CONTEXTUALIZED ECCLESIOLOGICALLY   73
CENTERED ON JESUS CHRIST, THE WISDOM OF GOD   77
GROUNDED IN SCRIPTURE   80
CARRIED OUT AS A RE-CREATIVE PROCESS GUIDED BY THE SPIRIT   84
ORIENTED TOWARD THE REIGN OF GOD   86

4 | Reenvisioning pastoral counseling   91
A DISTINCTIVE WAY OF WALKING WITH OTHERS   91
AS THEY FACE LIFE'S CHALLENGES AND STRUGGLES   97
THAT THEY MAY LIVE WISELY IN THE LIGHT OF GOD   108
CONCLUSION   114

Selected bibliography   117

For Gabriella Carmen and Lucas Daniel,
my grandchildren:

May you grow in wisdom
in the light of God.

Gratitudes

The seed of this book was planted during a productive time I spent at the Center of Theological Inquiry, in Princeton. I am grateful for the opportunity I had to enjoy its wonderful resources for research, and for energizing conversation with fellow members of the center. A grant from the Louisville Institute made it possible to complete this writing project, thanks to the encouragement I received from Craig Dykstra, Vice President for Religion, The Lilly Endowment, and the counsel of the Institute's director, James Lewis.

Special thanks go to my colleagues in the two institutions of theological education where I have worked longest, Seminario Evangélico de Puerto Rico and Associated Mennonite Biblical Seminary. I am particularly indebted to a multitude of students through more than three decades, not only in those two schools but also in several other places in Latin America and the Caribbean, North America, and Europe. Further, I am grateful to so many counselees who welcomed me into their lives as they faced existential challenges and struggles in a variety of pastoral counseling settings and intercultural situations.

A number of colleagues have affirmed me vocationally in diverse ways, and several of them responded to earlier versions of this essay in one form or another. I am grateful to them all: Herbert Anderson, Homer Ashby, David Augsburger, Kathleen Billman, Don Browning, Donald Capps, Alvin C. Dueck, Delores Friesen, James Nelson Gingerich, Gerben Heitink, Carlos José Hernández, John Hershberger, Rodney Hunter, Loren Johns, Gayle Gerber Koontz, Marlene Kropf, Jorge León, Daniël Louw, David Lyall, Marianne Mellinger, Luis Fidel Mercado, Bonnie Miller-McLemore, Stephen Pattison, James N. Poling, John A. Rogers, Erik Sawatzky, Marcus Smucker, Jean Stairs, Willard Swartley, Erland Waltner, Perry Yoder, Lies Brussee–van der Zee, and others.

Throughout my life I have been blessed with the experience of church as special context of care and wisdom. I am grateful for the reality of faith communities that respond to the call to become sacraments of divine love in the world and for the sake of the world.

My thanks also go to five people who provided much needed assistance during the final phase of this writing project: Carole Boshart and Sue Conrad helped me generously as student and research assistants; Christine Guth provided editorial expertise essential for improving my writing style; Barbara Nelson Gingerich prepared the manuscript for publication in a diligent and efficient manner; and Mary Schertz, Institute of Mennonite Studies director, supplied oversight and wholehearted support for the project.

Finally, to my family I am especially grateful. Margaret Anne, my life partner, is a truly wise woman; and our little grand-children, to whom this book is dedicated, have brought new love, joy, and hope into my life.

DANIEL S. SCHIPANI

Elkhart, Indiana
Pentecost 2003

Introduction

THE DEVELOPMENT OF PASTORAL COUNSELING AS A specialized activity or separate profession within the larger domain of ministerial formation and pastoral practice has been something of a mixed blessing. On the one hand, the establishment of pastoral counseling centers and the growth of a population of trained, specialized pastoral counselors have placed pastors and other congregational caregivers in a quandary as far as this traditional art of Christian ministry is concerned. As Donald Capps asserts, pastors have found these developments intimidating or have viewed them as providing a defensible rationale for not engaging in much counseling themselves but instead leaving it to the "professionals."[1] From this perspective, pastoral ministers working in congregations must reclaim the essential role of pastoral counseling. On the other hand, those whom pastoral ministers serve have expected them to function as therapists in response to the desires, needs, and anxieties prevalent in our technological, militaristic, and therapeutic culture. William Willimon sheds light on this challenge in his recent discussion of pastoral ministry. The image of the pastor as therapist is problematic, he writes, unless *caring in the manner of Christ* determines the substance of that image and the consistent practice of pastoral care and counseling. Willimon argues in favor of reclaiming the ecclesial and theological base of pastoral care, and recovering "pastoral counseling as a means of spiritual

---

[1] Donald Capps, *Living Stories: Pastoral Counseling in Congregational Context* (Minneapolis: Fortress Press, 1998), preface and introduction. Capps also affirms the essential role of pastoral counseling in the life of the congregation in response to "a fundamental human need to give systematic, constructive attention to the way that individuals 'story' their lives [inspirationally, paradoxically, and miraculously] so that they may develop new, more fulfilling life stories" (viii). Capps argues in favor of a "paradigmatic revolution" by introducing a narrative approach to pastoral counseling that integrates biblical insights and individual and family systems models of therapy.

direction, a theologically grounded endeavor to equip the saints for the work of ministry, a form of catechesis for Christian growth."[2] He suggests that the overarching goal of pastoral counseling ought to be contributing to people's maturity in the light of Christ.[3] I propose that the appraisals of these well-known authors are complementary: the church needs to reconsider a ministry of counseling (Capps) that is truly pastoral (Willimon) in a fruitful and faithful manner.

PASTORAL COUNSELING IN CONTEXT

We must consider the potential contributions and limitations of pastoral counseling in light of the church's call to participate in the praxis of God—*missio Dei*—in the midst of history. This call presents challenges and opportunities that we must realize within the realities of the globalization process currently under way, with its political, economic, technological, and cultural dimensions.[4] Indeed, interconnected systems of communication, transportation, political organization, and economic activity are weaving our world together into a single global locality. Globalization is restructuring the ways we live in diverse areas such as sexuality, marriage and family life, and the socialization of youth.[5] The

---

[2] William H. Willimon, *Pastor: The Theology and Practice of Ordained Ministry* (Louisville: Abingdon Press, 2001), 178. See chapter 2, "Ministry for the Twenty-First Century: Images of the Pastor" (especially 59–61); chapter 4, "The Priest As Pastor: Worship As the Content and Context of Pastoral Care"; and chapter 7, "The Pastor As Counselor: Care That Is Christian."

[3] Ibid., 183.

[4] Globalization, rather than postmodernity, is the broad category intended. Robert J. Schreiter has argued convincingly that the investigation of the very future of theology is best done, not within the framework of "postmodernism" (which would provide mainly an interaction with symptoms), but within the larger framework of globalization. See his *The New Catholicity: Theology between the Global and the Local* (Maryknoll: Orbis Books, 1997), especially chapter 1.

[5] See, for instance, Anthony Giddens, *Runaway World: How Globalization Is Reshaping Our Lives* (New York: Routledge, 2000). Giddens insightfully discusses the new faces of risk, the transformation of tradition and democracy, and the changes affecting our personal lives, with a very accessible style. For a comprehensive introduction to the subject of globalization, see David Held, Anthony McGrew, David Goldblatt, and Jonathan Perraton, *Global*

influence of the dominant global market–capitalist system is pervasive, and its supporting ideology powerfully conditions our social and cultural situation.[6] Those of us living in the United States must acknowledge that globalization is led from the West and bears the strong imprint of American political and economic power, currently further supported by aggressive militarism.[7] These many interwoven elements combine to form the context in which pastoral counseling takes place.

From the New Testament we receive the conviction that God intends the church to be unified, a single communion. In our modern context, we may interpret this to mean a global, transnational communion that remains incarnationally grounded in the manifold regional, national, and local contexts where it lives and ministers. This conviction implies that the church accepts a vocation of partnership with God for the sake of the world. This vocation supplies the larger vision of care in the manner of Christ that inspires my work.

THE REASON FOR THIS BOOK

My research and writing in the area of pastoral care[8] during recent years has sought a creative and constructive response to two

---

Transformations: Politics, Economics, and Culture (Cambridge, U.K.: Polity Press, 1999).

[6] Ethicist Cynthia D. Moe-Lobeda offers an incisive critique of the disabling power, especially in terms of moral agency, of global economic arrangements requiring us to exploit rather than to love both Earth and neighbor. She also proposes ways of resistance and hope by addressing how faith in (and of) Jesus Christ might enable moral agency to resist those arrangements and to forge alternatives. See her book, *Healing a Broken World: Globalization and God* (Minneapolis: Fortress Press, 2002).

[7] As the sole superpower, the United States has recently embraced a doctrine of preventive war and insists on absolute freedom of action in the context of its global power projection. As a matter of policy, the U.S. is now committed to maintaining its present military supremacy in perpetuity; military force has become the main instrument of American statecraft. The consequences of these developments will certainly affect our lives in new ways in the years ahead.

[8] *Pastoral care* may be defined as including "those activities of the Church which are directed towards maintaining or restoring the health and wholeness of individuals and communities in the context of God's redemptive purposes for all creation" (Alastair V. Campbell, "Pastoral Care," in *The New Dictionary of Pastoral*

interrelated problems I have encountered in the field of pastoral counseling,[9] including its experiential, practical, and theoretical dimensions. The first of these problems I outlined at the beginning of this introduction. It consists of a sense of incompetence on the part of many pastoral caregivers in the face of pastoral counseling clinical specialization and professional certification. The second problem I perceive is a lack of direction and internal coherence within pastoral counseling as a distinct ministry art and as a dimension of the wider field of pastoral care. This deficit includes a lack of congruence and continuity between pastoral counseling and other ministry arts, especially teaching, preaching, mentoring,

---

Studies, ed. Wesley Carr [Grand Rapids: Eerdmans, 2002], 252–3). When broadly and inclusively viewed in this way, pastoral care is that dimension of the ministry of the church that is concerned with the well-being of individuals and communities. It may include various functions—such as guiding, nurturing, sustaining, reconciling, and healing—in diverse modes and settings, including those of pastoral counseling.

[9] *Pastoral counseling* is commonly viewed as a specialized dimension of pastoral care. A brief consensus definition would be: pastoral counseling is a form of pastoral care for a person, couple, family, or small group, extended by agreement or contract over a period of time, with a relatively definite goal. Howard Clinebell describes its uniqueness as "derived from the training of pastors that equips them to integrate insights from contemporary psychosocial sciences and psychotherapeutic methods, on the one hand, with the healing resources of the Jewish and Christian heritages and the resources of gathered communities of faith, on the other" (in *The New Dictionary of Pastoral Studies,* ed. Carr, 253–4). Some authors further characterize pastoral counseling in terms of their theological traditions, as illustrated by David W. Ausgburger. Augsburger highlights three characteristics of pastoral counseling grounded in Anabaptist theology, as counseling that stresses: "1) embeddedness in the faith community, which is the context of pastoral care; 2) the integration of both the therapeutic and the ethical dynamics of intrapersonal and interpersonal conflicts; 3) the unity of personal, familial, social, national, and global aspects of peacemaking and the creation of shalom. Thus the pastoral counselor in the Mennonite context seeks to nurture healing relationships within the healing community; to clarify health and wholeness as well as justice and ethically right relationships; to invite reconciliation with oneself, one's significant others and the larger community." In *Mennonite Encyclopedia,* ed. Cornelius J. Dyck and Dennis D. Martin (Scottdale: Herald Press, 1990) 5:675–6. I present and discuss a comprehensive redefinition of pastoral counseling in detail in chapter 4.

and spiritual guidance.[10] My research has consisted primarily in an exploration of the practical theological nature of pastoral counseling. Indeed, I conceive and design my work as a critical and constructive endeavor in pastoral and practical theology.[11]

I work with the assumption that these two problems in the pastoral counseling field relate directly to the continuing predominance of the clinical[12] and existentialist-anthropological[13]

---

[10] The two interrelated problems I highlight are especially significant from a theological standpoint. It is possible to identify additional challenges and opportunities for correction, renewal, and redirection in the field, most of which have been articulated in the last several years by different authors. For example, two fine, still pertinent, critical appraisals by British contributors are: Alastair Campbell, *Professionalism and Pastoral Care* (Philadelphia: Fortress Press, 1985); and Stephen Pattison, *A Critique of Pastoral Care* (London: SCM Press, 1988). Ghanaian pastoral theologian Emmanuel Y. Lartey summarizes the critique of pastoral counseling in terms of problems related to a western approach to pastoral care: psychological reductionism (including professional-clinical captivity), social and political apathy, theological weakness (including deficiencies in ethics and spirituality), and individualism (Lartey, *In Living Color: An Intercultural Approach to Pastoral Care and Counseling,* 2d ed. [London and New York: Jessica Kingsley Publications, 2003], 108–11).

[11] *Pastoral theology* is usually understood in North America, within Protestant churches, as theological inquiry into the ministry of care, broadly and inclusively viewed, as I indicated in footnote 8 above. Pastoral theology thus contributes theoretical understandings as well as practical guidelines for the church's ministry of care. Pastoral theology is therefore considered a major dimension of the larger field and discipline of *practical* theology (which, in turn, may be understood as critical and constructive reflection on the life and ministry of the church—with special focus on formation and transformation—in terms of the sociohistorical context and in the light of God's reign). Within the Roman Catholic Church, pastoral theology is a broader concept (sometimes also called practical theology) that refers to the theology, education, and practices of ordained priests working in parishes, including sacraments, liturgy, preaching, teaching, and counseling. See James N. Poling, "Pastoral Theology," in *The New Dictionary of Pastoral Studies,* ed. Carr, 258–9.

[12] For a survey of the trajectory of the clinical pastoral education movement— which has directly led to the establishment of the clinical paradigm—and its widespread success in the training of pastoral caregivers, see Edward E. Thornton, "Clinical Pastoral Education," in *Dictionary of Pastoral Care and Counseling,* ed. Rodney Hunter (Nashville: Abingdon Press, 1990), 177–82.

[13] For this description of the current dominant paradigm as existentialist-anthropological, I am indebted to Larry K. Graham, *Care of Persons, Care of*

paradigm, including its psychotherapeutic model, in pastoral counseling. This clinical pastoral paradigm has been in place for more than fifty years. Its foremost contribution has consisted in focusing on the people in counseling and illuminating the dynamics of their relationships. At its best, pastoral counseling draws from the clinical paradigm the use of both psychological and theological resources to deepen its understanding of caregiver and care-receiver and the relationship between them. In addition to providing insights on process and on the pastoral and therapeutic relationship as a unique setting for care and healing, the clinical model contributes significantly to our understanding of personality and human development from a psychodynamic perspective (for instance by focusing on intrapersonal and interpersonal conflict, and the theory of the unconscious).

The clinical paradigm becomes problematic to the extent that the word *clinical*—originally referring to medical practice at the sick bed—defines the practice of pastoral counseling in the reductionist terms of a medical model mainly concerned with pathology. When that happens, pastoral counseling is viewed, practiced, and taught primarily as psychotherapy. One can easily observe the dominance of this medical and psychiatric model. Pastoral counselors use extensively the language of psychopathology and mental health or emotional adjustment, they rely on standard diagnostic tools, and they pattern their practice after professional psychotherapy (with licensing that regulates the practice, and certification that legitimates a distinct professional identity under state law). Under the determining influence of psychotherapy, pastoral counseling has become increasingly specialized; indeed, pastoral counseling has too often been viewed, practiced, and taught as if it were merely a subtype within the psychotherapy industry. Pastoral counseling thus framed has become the dominant mode of pastoral care. No wonder the influential American Association of Pastoral Counselors, founded in 1963, identifies pastoral counselors as

---

Worlds: Psychosystems Approach to Pastoral Care and Counseling (Nashville: Abingdon Press, 1992), 14.

certified mental health professionals who have had in-depth religious and/or theological training.[14]

The reason I challenge this clinical-medical paradigm is that it draws too heavily on individualistic psychological theories and existentialist-based theologies and philosophies. In theological terms, it is ordered primarily by anthropological considerations. Further, the prevailing paradigm tends to focus on intrapsychic dynamics, with autonomy and self-realization as its primary goals; it assumes that individuals and their primary groups may somehow fashion fulfilling lives largely in spite of the actual realities of culture, society, and nature. Thus, together with its inadequate theological grounding, the model provides insufficient attention to and engagement with the ecclesial and historical-cultural context in which pastoral care ministry takes place.

In light of these interrelated problems, it is fitting to propose a significant shift regarding pastoral counseling. My proposal, outlined in this book, will address the context, foundations, and specific practical guidelines for pastoral counseling as a ministry of the church.

THESIS AND SCOPE

My thesis is that pastoral counseling, a special dimension and form of pastoral care, must be reconsidered from a practical theological perspective as a special setting and process for the practice of wisdom. Therefore, pastoral counseling must be reframed; it must be viewed, practiced, and taught in a new and different framework. Its normative biblical and theological base must be affirmed and stated afresh. I further propose that we can accomplish this reframing well by reclaiming wisdom (wisdom in the light of God, that is) as the master metaphor for pastoral counseling. My research, grounded in practice, confirms this understanding as a useful way to reenvision pastoral counseling as a special form of ministry. *Wisdom in the light of God* supplies a

---

14 The American Association of Pastoral Counselors (AAPC) certifies pastoral counselors, accredits pastoral counseling centers, and approves training programs. It represents and sets professional standards for more than 3,000 pastoral counselors and 100 counseling centers in the United States. People become members of AAPC through a process of consultation and review of academic and clinical education.

guiding principle to reclaim and strengthen the theological and epistemological foundations of pastoral counseling as a ministry of the church while reaffirming unique aspects of pastoral counseling as a form of counseling. Below I outline the content of the four chapters that support my thesis and make up this book.

In the first chapter, "Reflecting on the practice of pastoral counseling," I provide specific illustrations from my pastoral counseling practice. Summaries of case studies focus on psychological and theological perspectives and the need to consider multiple dimensions of experience. These cases also illustrate objectives of pastoral counseling in the service of discernment, nurture and guidance, support, reconciliation, and healing. Here I demonstrate the possibility of moving beyond the prevailing medical model while tracing the contours of a new interpretive framework based on wisdom (instead of mental health) as the ground metaphor for pastoral counseling. A final section of the chapter introduces an emerging vision, drawn from the perspective of practical theology, that constructively focuses the question: What makes pastoral counseling the kind of counseling that is truly pastoral? To conclude the chapter, I propose that pastoral counseling aims at awakening, nurturing, and developing people's moral and spiritual intelligence—their ability to live well and wisely in the face of life's challenges and struggles.

The second chapter, "Reclaiming wisdom as the heart," presents theological foundations from the biblical wisdom tradition that culminates in Jesus Christ and the promise of new life in the Spirit. Here I spell out my central claim that wisdom addresses certain fundamental existential questions: How shall we live in conformity with the culture of the reign of God? How shall we together make the kind of world that pleases God? I emphasize the continuity and complementarity between counseling and other ministry art forms, and the pastoral character of pastoral counseling. The chapter discusses the intimate connection between the biblical motifs of the reign of God and wisdom—the rich and multifaceted biblical wisdom tradition as a way of doing theology—and Jesus Christ, the wisdom of God. Finally, I focus on how to relate the way of wisdom to the ministry art of pastoral counseling.

When wisdom constitutes the overall guiding principle of pastoral counseling, as it has in my research, it leads to a new conceptualization of this ministry art. Therefore, the content of my third chapter, "Reframing pastoral counseling," growing out of my research, consists of a detailed response to the question: What happens, practically speaking, when the theological base of pastoral counseling is reaffirmed and this ministry art is reframed in terms of wisdom in the light of God? I propose that reframing pastoral counseling as the way of wisdom in the light of God calls for the appropriation of normative guidelines which characterize it as a ministry of the church. The groups of guidelines I have developed focus in turn on the following six characteristics of pastoral counseling in the wisdom framework. Such counseling is (a) viewed, practiced, and taught pastorally; (b) contextualized ecclesiologically; (c) centered on Jesus Christ as the wisdom of God; (d) grounded in Scripture; (e) viewed, practiced, and taught as a unique form of the re-creative process guided by the Spirit; and (f) oriented toward the reign of God.

The fourth chapter, "Reenvisioning pastoral counseling," presents a detailed, illustrated explanation of the following definition: Pastoral counseling is a special art and form of ministry of the church. In pastoral counseling, human emergence is uniquely sponsored by a distinctive way of walking with others— whether individuals, couples, family members, or small groups— as they face life's challenges and struggles; the overall goal, simply stated, is that they may live wisely in the light of God. In support of this definition, I propose five overarching guidelines, presented here in summary form. (1) The primary concern in pastoral counseling must be to help people live wholesome and faithful lives in the midst of normal human journeys. (2) Pastoral counseling must recover its function and value as a ministry of guidance and discernment, through challenging people to practice good judgment, to choose well, and to make wise decisions in a wide variety of life dimensions and situations. (3) It must also focus on healing broken relationships; pastoral counselors have a unique opportunity to participate in the reconciliation ministry that God has entrusted to the Christian faith community. (4) Pastoral counselors can also play a key role in the face of the natural vulnerabilities of human life, including difficult transitions, developmental and accidental crises, sickness, loss, and death; they must do so by participating in various forms of supportive and healing ministry. (5) Last but not least, we must recover the noble tradition of pastoral care and counseling as a form of Christian service that is especially available to marginalized, victimized, poor, and oppressed people, while working toward communal and social transformation.

FINAL WORDS

This is not a book on how to do pastoral counseling. Rather, it is about re-viewing pastoral counseling with practical theological lenses. Thus, I invite readers to ponder an alternative way of seeing and talking about pastoral counseling that has significant implications for the practice and teaching of this art of ministry in the larger field of pastoral care.

Finally, a word about why I chose the title *The Way of Wisdom in Pastoral Counseling*. The phrase deliberately includes two connotations. First, the term *wisdom* connotes a holistic way of knowing, which includes discerning, making good choices, and living well in community. Second, the phrase *in pastoral counseling* implies that other forms and settings of ministry similarly foster the way of wisdom for our daily life. The way of wisdom must also define the nature and the goals of these other practices of ministry, such as teaching, preaching, spiritual guidance, mentoring, and youth ministry. Ultimately, the aims of these ministry practices converge with pastoral counseling in the direction of guiding others—as well as being guided—toward wholeness and fullness of life in the light of the gospel of the reign of God.

1 | *Reflecting on the practice*

I N THE INTRODUCTION, I ARGUED THAT PASTORAL COUNSELING must be reconsidered, from the perspective of practical theology, as a special setting and process for the practice of wisdom. Since practical theology points to human experience in the real world as a starting point for our discussion, a large part of this chapter consists of case studies in pastoral counseling. These cases function like windows through which we can see various aspects of the pastoral counseling experience. I examine four cases dealing with diverse dimensions of human existence, offer psychological and theological perspectives that illuminate counseling themes, and summarize specific pastoral counseling goals with focus on care-seekers and the caregiver. The final part of the chapter presents an emerging vision for pastoral counseling, also from the perspective of practical theology.

FOUR WINDOWS TO PASTORAL COUNSELING

Summaries of pastoral counseling situations selected from my practice illustrate dimensions or emphases of the pastoral counseling process.[1] Each of these dimensions—discernment, guidance, nurture, support, reconciliation, healing, liberating—is always present in some measure, although one normally focuses on one or a few of them. In these cases, as in others, I have been intentional about working in a pastoral care framework, because I believe that pastoral counseling must be practiced, reflected on, and taught primarily as a special form and setting of pastoral caregiving, even when it takes place outside congregational

---

[1] Each of the four cases represents situations I have actually encountered in pastoral counseling. For the sake of clarity, I have chosen cases whose resolution was fully satisfactory from the counselees' perspectives as well as from my own. Readers may keep in mind that here, and elsewhere in this book, I present composites in order to preserve confidentiality.

boundaries.[2] Further, I have made an effort to integrate perspectives and contributions from various sources, such as the human sciences (especially psychology) and theology.[3] I have kept these concerns in mind while attending to the unique needs of each pastoral counseling situation in its own social and cultural context. Most importantly, as I have counseled others I have remained aware of my call to become a faithful and fruitful mediator of divine grace and wisdom.

After presenting a summary of each counseling situation, I have outlined the pastoral counseling agenda as I perceived it through psychological and theological lenses, as counseling unfolded in each of these four cases. One must view the resulting sets of issues focused by the two lenses as inseparable, however. I also include succinct statements of the goals that we pursued in each pastoral counseling case.

CALVIN: REFOCUSING IDENTITY AND VOCATION

Calvin was a recently retired pastor in his late sixties. He had been experiencing signs of depression (feeling persistently sad and empty, with diminished interest in activities he had previously enjoyed, difficulty making decisions, etc.). His family doctor had prescribed antidepressant medication and encouraged him to discuss his situation with a pastoral counselor. Calvin had been an active and productive ministering person during most of his adult life. He had struggled with adjusting to the status of retiree, but had begun to invest his considerable experience and competence in volunteer work, including some church-related assignments. The pastoral counseling agenda included, first, determining

---

[2] As I stated in the introduction, I do not subscribe to the medical/psychiatric view of pastoral counseling. Within that framework, pastoral counseling is treated as a subtype of the psychotherapy industry, and pastoral counselors are considered mental health professionals.

[3] By *integration* I do not mean, for example, the integration of psychology and theology as such, because that effort would be logically inappropriate. On the contrary, the distinctive integrity of each discipline must be maintained even as we learn from, evaluate, contribute to, and apply them, side by side. The theoretical and practical integration that really matters must be embodied in us as ministering people; this embodiment includes the critical appropriation of personal and pastoral-professional experience.

whether Calvin's depression was primarily a reaction to the losses involved in his professional transition or a condition requiring specialized medical assistance, and second, processing the interrelated issues of identity and family, faith and vocation.

Calvin was entering a new chapter in his life as a senior citizen and retiree. He needed to reshape his personal and vocational identity after many years of fruitful pastoral ministry. He also needed to discover a fresh sense of integrity and self-worth. As a newly retired person, Calvin was experiencing significant changes in his social world. His sense of time, his relationships, and his opportunities for work and leisure were being affected by the changes in his role in the community, church, and family. Thus, Calvin's distress and disorientation involved several aspects of his self and his lived world.[4]

Calvin was confronting faces of the void, the threat of nonbeing, directly connected to real losses he already felt. Further, he was anticipating additional losses in sense of purpose and meaning, and possibly overall well-being and health. On the other hand, he could also sense, however dimly, the possibility of new being by the grace of God, a possibility that became conceivable through his confrontation with the void. Somehow, he could hope, the darkness reflected in his depression would be transformed into a new experience of light and love—that is, the negation of the negation—effected by the one who had called him in the first place and would forever keep him whole and safe.

Specifics of the pastoral counseling agenda. Calvin and I agreed he needed to address some interrelated issues connected with the termination of his regular ministerial occupation:

- the loss of a regular job, with the attendant loss of role and status as pastoral leader in a congregation;

---

[4] In each of the initial summaries of the cases I locate the situation by using James E. Loder's view of "the fourfold knowing event"—which involves the lived world, the self, the void, and the Holy. See *The Transforming Moment*, 2d ed. (Colorado Springs: Helmers & Howard, 1989), chapter 3. Loder writes that "being human entails environment, selfhood, the possibility of not being, and the possibility of new being. All four dimensions are essential, and none of them can be ignored without decisive loss to our understanding of what is essentially human" (69).

- significant changes related to self-identity and vocation, coupled with possible changes in marriage and family life (resulting from having more unstructured time and a reduced monthly income);
- the need to express and process his grief well, and to discern the sources and nature of his depression;
- moving from personal and vocational disorientation to reorientation while attending to issues of aging and health.

From a more explicitly pastoral theological perspective several closely related themes became the focus of our consideration, by mutual agreement:

- o personal spirituality (relationship with God since retirement; rediscovering the joy of being a child of God);
- o ministerial vocation and divine grace beyond active, fruitful pastoring, including issues related to continued participation in the life of a faith community;
- o grieving in the light of God, including consideration of lament, reappraisal, freedom, gratitude, peace, hope, and recommitment;
- o refocusing on fruits of the Spirit and maturing love of God, others, and self, including spiritual resources to sustain love in the months ahead.

Pastoral counseling goals. In Calvin's case, as in my other pastoral counseling cases, I sought to remain aware of two sets of objectives. In addition to the goals articulated by counselees (or negotiated with them in light of their perceived needs or reasons for seeking counseling), I set objectives for myself as a pastoral counselor. The two sets of goals are certainly related.

Calvin and I first agreed on specific goals he would pursue with my guidance:

- to explore issues of identity and vocation, including relationship with himself, God, and others (especially his spouse and family and the faith community);
- to revisit his life story and faith journey in the light of Scripture and the gospel, with an eye toward rekindling hope;
- to gain a new spiritual sense of "restful reliance" (an expression that Calvin received as an insight) on divine

grace and providence, while also seeking to develop new spiritual disciplines;

- to refashion a sense of self-worth, meaning, and purpose in the light of faith, and from that base to make wise choices that would shape life in the years to come.

Second, as I entered a counseling relationship with Calvin, I knew that I was primarily responsible for meeting goals of my own, such as these:[5]

□ to welcome Calvin in a safe and caring space where he could express himself freely (particularly in light of the fact that I was a younger colleague and ministering person who needed to communicate special respect to him);

□ to represent the healing Christ and the church as a community of care and wisdom; to mediate divine grace as Calvin moved from the disorientation linked to retirement toward reorientation;

□ to become, for a short while, a companion in Calvin's journey toward reorientation and renewal (by listening well, comforting, guiding him in a discerning process, helping him communicate with God and make wise decisions, and holding him accountable);

□ to minister as a caregiving sage who would practice pastoral counseling competently (for example, by introducing *cognitive restructuring*[6] to help Calvin perceive his world more realistically and change misconceptions and expectations directly connected with his depression; this in turn would help determine whether Calvin's depression would require specialized medical assistance).

---

[5] Because most of the goals I set for myself as a pastoral counselor apply, in principle, to most pastoral counseling situations, I will not repeat them in the discussion of the remaining three cases. Nevertheless, the reader should remember that they are implied.

[6] As a counseling intervention, cognitive restructuring is a broadly used method associated with cognitive psychotherapies. It is employed to help people change their learned negative cognitions and to teach them more realistic sets of beliefs, including the practice of reformulating irrational thoughts in light of a new vision of reality.

KATHY: LEARNING TO LIVE WITHOUT DAD

Kathy was a sixteen year old whose father had died recently and unexpectedly in a traffic accident. The trauma had been particularly hard for her as the youngest member of the family and "daddy's girl." She was struggling with the tension generated by anger toward God and her desire to find consolation in her faith. She also faced conflicting feelings and many questions, including lingering doubts about whether her father had caused the accident that took his life. The resulting crisis exacerbated the anxieties associated with developmental issues adolescent girls normally face (self-image, sexuality, friendships, values, and religion, and an emerging sense of vocational direction). Further, Kathy's situation occurred in the context of the grieving process under way in the rest of the family, and especially, that of her mother. Supportive pastoral counseling soon led to considering interconnected questions of family, friends, faith, and the church.

Kathy was coping with the major trauma of the unexpected death of her father in a car accident. At the time of the crisis, she was working out her sense of identity, and her teenage self was still in flux and formation. She had been dealing with questions of love, friendship and family relationships, study and vocation, the body and sexuality, faith and values. That process had taken place normally, in the settings of school, peer interactions, church, and family. Now the family, which had been a place of comfort and guidance, had changed dramatically because of her father's absence and because of the grief Kathy, her two siblings, and their mother were experiencing.

The death of a loving parent abruptly confronted Kathy with one of the worst faces of the void. Along with deep sadness, she felt anxiety associated with the uncertain future of the family. The void with its great pain caused her to question the love and the power of God. Yet in releasing her anger she was also seeking to be embraced by the divine grace that reaches beyond despair. Somehow, Kathy realized, she needed to draw comfort, strength, and direction from the spiritual wellsprings of her faith and her church. In due time, hope and peace would prevail.

Specifics of the pastoral counseling agenda. Key interrelated issues Kathy and I needed to consider together in the counseling relationship included:

- deep grief, including a degree of anger and ambivalence toward her father (for example, she wondered to what extent he had been responsible for the accident);
- developmental steps in the grief work that would take her toward healing: from accepting the reality of the tragic loss of her father and expressing painful feelings, to finding ways of coping and reinvesting life energy;
- significant changes in the family system, including reconfiguring relationships with mother and siblings, shifting roles, and new financial challenges for the family;
- the ways this accidental crisis of sudden loss of her father affected Kathy's normal developmental crisis as an adolescent girl in high school;
- availability of resources to support Kathy during the bereavement process and beyond.

In addition to those and related issues, the explicitly pastoral and theological perspective from which I work as a caregiver raised significant concerns. Thus, from the beginning of the counseling relationship, Kathy and I considered these key themes:

- o anger toward God, with questions related to Kathy's images of God and her views on divine will, power, mercy, and justice;
- o the reality and the mystery surrounding death, and Kathy's awakened sense of her own mortality and vulnerability;
- o the meaning and function of her Christian faith in the face of tragic loss and trauma; the place and role of beliefs, for example, about the human spirit and the afterlife, and practices, such as prayer;
- o the potential for spiritual growth as she would confront the crisis and eventually resolve it wisely.

Pastoral counseling goals. In light of Kathy's felt needs, we agreed to work toward certain objectives, so that Kathy would be helped:

- ▪ to accept, understand, and start integrating her sense of loss through the normal multifaceted and painful process of grief, in the light of faith;

- to activate available resources, both internal and external, in order to cope with the crisis and its ramifications on the personal and family levels, in wholesome ways;
- to strengthen her sense of personal identity, integrity, and security within the larger framework of Christian spiritual formation and transformation;
- to develop and begin to implement a plan for further bereavement work, including adjustments to life without her father.

As I indicated earlier in the case of Calvin, the goals I set for myself—welcoming in a safe place, representing the healing Christ and the care and wisdom of the faith community, accompanying, and ministering as a wise caregiver—apply to other pastoral counseling situations, including my work with Kathy. More specifically, however, my aim of counseling Kathy competently involved applying understandings as well as methodological resources commonly associated with the strategies of crisis, supportive, and bereavement pastoral care and counseling.[7] Therefore, key objectives for my caregiving endeavors included the following:

- to become a supportive presence and a source of spiritual comfort by listening responsively, encouraging catharsis, and making available resources from diverse sources (the human sciences, the Christian faith tradition and local faith community, and others) to sustain Kathy's grief work;
- to help Kathy cope with and make decisions in the face of the new realities in her life, and to guide her in reality testing;
- to sponsor her spiritual growth by encouraging her participation in communal faith practices and development of spiritual disciplines;
- to enable her outreach to others, especially to those who might extend continuing support to Kathy and her family

---

[7] For descriptions and illustrations of supportive, crisis, and bereavement care and counseling, see Howard Clinebell, *Basic Types of Pastoral Care and Counseling: Resources for the Ministry of Healing and Growth* (Nashville: Abingdon Press, 1984), chapters 7, 8, and 9, respectively. See also David K. Switzer, *The Minister As Crisis Counselor*, rev. ed. (Nashville: Abingdon Press, 1986); and Howard W. Stone, *Crisis Counseling*, rev. ed. (Minneapolis: Fortress Press, 1993).

beyond short-term pastoral counseling, primarily in the context of the faith community.

JUDY AND ROBERT: REENVISIONING PARENTING AND MARRIAGE

Judy and Robert were both in their mid-forties and had been married for twenty-one years. Their nineteen-year-old son, Richard, had recently fallen in love with an older woman, Lydia, whom he had met via the internet. Soon after Richard and Lydia met in person, they became sexually involved, and according to Richard, were considering marriage in the near future. Judy and Robert disapproved of the relationship because they felt their son was not ready for marriage, let alone for marriage to this woman, whom they had met, awkwardly, only once. Judy was particularly worried about the issue of premarital sexual relations as sinful, and felt guilty about her son's choices. Robert and Judy said they did not know how to deal with their son. In addition to addressing issues of how to relate to Richard, and views on sin and moral responsibility, pastoral counseling uncovered a need for Judy and Robert to work on communication dynamics in their own marriage.

Judy and Robert were respected members of their church and community. They had enjoyed a relatively peaceful life as a couple and family, and their jobs (part-time in Judy's case) were fulfilling. Their identities had been primarily defined in terms of their self-understanding as Christian parents and spouses, and they had not had to face any major family crisis until Richard told them about his relationship with Lydia and his plans to marry her. Suddenly their world was shaken.

For Judy and Robert, encountering the void meant that with the possibility of "losing" a son they were facing a twofold threat. First, they were afraid that Richard would make bad choices with serious, lifelong consequences, especially entering unwisely into marriage. Second, they were feeling impotent and regretful, with a sense of failure and inadequacy as Christian parents, which was a defining vocation and role for them. The possibility that all was not well with their marriage conveyed additional anxiety. Therefore, the void also presented the specters of sin and guilt. Yet their anguish concealed a potential for transformation. On the one hand, they could be helped psychologically, in the two-dimensional framework of self and the lived world (in recomposing their selves, their relationship, and their family world in adaptive ways). On the other hand, pastoral counseling could assist them to confront the void while embracing divine wisdom and power, resulting in a more holistic or transformational healing (drawing on James Loder's four-dimensional view). Stated more concretely, Judy and Robert's struggle could become an occasion for comprehensive personal, relational, and spiritual renewal.[8]

Specifics of the pastoral counseling agenda. Judy's and Robert's differing versions of the family crisis made it clear that we would need to focus on several issues that may be illuminated using the perspectives and contributions of the practical human sciences, particularly psychology and counseling/psychotherapy:

- Judy and Robert's concern about Richard's emotional immaturity, and the possibility of relating to him as a young adult responsible for his actions and choices (while letting go of him as a dependent child);
- the particular nature of system and family dynamics, including the exploration of roles, expectations, and communication patterns;
- issues of parenting, and ways to relate to their son, and possibly, to Lydia;
- the specific dynamics of their marriage (ways of relating and communcating) now being tested in response to Richard's choices.

Judy and Robert expected a pastoral care approach to their current life struggle, an approach that I would have used in any

---

[8] Loder discusses this distinction and connection. For example, in commenting on the combination of the psychological and transformational movements in a personal instance of depression, he writes: "The *psychological* movement is the undoing of the depression. Based on aggression against oneself, depression may be relieved by externalization in anger. . . . The *transformational* movement includes the psychological dynamic but, employing a wider frame of reference, it turns the depression into an occasion for finding the ultimate ground of the self. . . . Psychology is interested primarily in adaptation, while transformation of the self works to redeem the significance of the whole sequence, including the depression, as a passage-way to centeredness in the Holy" (*The Transforming Moment*, 88–9).

event. Therefore, my pastoral theological perspective in the counseling work informed our focusing explicitly on these pertinent issues:

- o parental responsibilities in the light of God, especially guilt in the face of presumed failure to measure up to standards of good, Christian parenting;
- o clarifying when behavior may be properly considered sinful (including the possible distinction between *sinful* and *unwise* choices, as in the case of premarital sexual relations) and exploring dimensions of forgiveness;
- o discerning how to mediate divine grace and wisdom to each other, and especially to their son and his lover;
- o identifying and appropriating spiritual resources for further support and guidance.

Pastoral counseling goals. Judy's special need for assistance that she shared with me in an initial interview contributed provisionally toward setting objectives. We then revised these objectives in light of Robert's input in a second, joint session. The shared objectives included these:

- ▪ to understand clearly the nature of their struggle and to deal with their emotions and feelings of anxiety, confusion, and inadequacy in the light of faith;
- ▪ to find ways to relate and communicate better with Richard (especially how to freely express love and care as well as concern), and to explore the possibility of reaching out to Lydia;
- ▪ to identify other sources of moral and spiritual nurture and support, beyond pastoral counseling;
- ▪ to make a plan to enrich their own marriage, including participation in a church-sponsored marriage enrichment program in the area.

My pastoral counseling approach with Judy and Robert was oriented toward these same objectives but from the perspective of counselor. I needed to guide a process of pastoral care that included dimensions of supportive and crisis counseling, and potentially, marriage enrichment. Therefore, as a pastoral caregiver, in addition to the general goals I outlined for the previous cases, my objectives were:

- ☐ to support Judy and Robert in differentiating themselves from their son's choices and behavior while helping them understand their family and marriage dynamics;
- ☐ to provide moral guidance from the perspective of the Christian faith, in the face of uncertainty about moral responsibility (their own and Richard's);
- ☐ to make available to them resources to improve communication and conflict resolution skills in their marriage and in their relationship with Richard; to offer my ministry to them (and perhaps to Richard as well) as a possible agent for peacemaking and reconciliation;
- ☐ to provide pastoral and spiritual support, especially by helping them embrace divine grace and seek divine wisdom.

PEDRO AND SONIA: BECOMING RESPONSIBLE LOVERS

Pedro was a soft-spoken twenty-one year old. He was referred to me because he needed a Spanish-speaking counselor, and because he preferred to talk with a married man about his concerns. Pedro's stated problem had to do primarily with sexuality issues. He and his seventeen-year-old girlfriend, Sonia, were becoming intimately involved. As they tried to begin a sexual relationship, both experienced difficulty connected with a sense of guilt. Pedro also said that he was having performance anxieties. The two were Roman Catholic and participated in mass sporadically. During the first counseling session it became apparent that Pedro and Sonia were misinformed about key facts of human sexuality (for instance, Pedro assumed that Sonia would not became pregnant unless they experienced orgasm simultaneously). The following three sessions of counseling, including two with Sonia, focused on providing orientation, as well as moral and spiritual guidance.

Pedro and Sonia were two young people learning to live in the intersection of the Latino-Mexican culture and the culture of the American Midwest. Although their English language skills were still limited, they were clearly joining the ranks of the millions of dual-culture or "hybrid"[9] individuals living in the

---

[9] The adjective *hybrid* is sometimes used by Latino scholars in reference to the social and cultural condition of Latin American and Caribbean people who

United States. Their personal identities were being shaped by the social reality of two differing cultures. Although their experiences of family, friendships, study (high school in Sonia's case), work, leisure, and play still had a primarily Mexican flavor, it was apparent that they were becoming Americanized.

By the time we started with pastoral counseling, Pedro and Sonia were struggling both individually and as a couple in connection with their wish to become sexually involved with each other. They were anxious about sexual activity as such; they were also anxious about not meeting family expectations (young women remain virgins until marriage; and a serious dating relationship does not include sexual intercourse, at least not so soon) and about disregarding the teachings of the Roman Catholic Church on human sexuality. They had questions about their bodies and sexual functioning, and at a deeper level, about the nature of intimacy and love. Further, these existential questions were uniquely shaped for each of them by the threat of the void in the specific forms of fear of impotence and loss of face, loss of virginity, and shame and guilt. Pastoral counseling would offer Pedro and Sonia more than the possibility of neutralizing negative emotions, or adjusting to cultural expectations and religious teaching (that is, psychological or two-dimensional solutions). It would also encourage them to embrace divine grace and be transformed by it.

Specifics of the pastoral counseling agenda. Pedro had taken the initiative to seek counseling before he was referred to me. Pedro raised certain issues; these were augmented by Sonia's concerns and by concerns the two of them shared. These included:

- Pedro's anxiety about sexuality, and particularly about his adequacy as a male in Hispanic culture; his anxiety directly connected with difficulties he was experiencing in

---

immigrate to the United States and eventually realize that they do not fully belong in either this country or their country of origin. They are constantly reminded of their status as outsiders because of their appearance, their accent, and certain social and cultural characteristics. As one who was born and grew up in Argentina and who maintains strong relationships and collaborative ties there and elsewhere in Latin America and the Caribbean, I claim this experience as a large part of my life story and identity.

sexual relations with Sonia (who happened to be a minor, a fact with potential legal ramifications);

- Sonia's specific anxieties as an adolescent Hispanic woman, including fear of their casual sexual activity being discovered by her parents, and of becoming pregnant;
- Pedro's and Sonia's apparent sense of shame and guilt associated with their sexual involvement, compounded by misinformation;
- their views of themselves as a young man and an adolescent woman, in light of their culturally conditioned notions of manhood and womanhood; their view of the nature and future of their relationship as a couple, in the context of their families and circle of friends.

These and related issues needed consideration also from a pastoral theological perspective, although that was not the expectation of these counselees. (They would have expected an explicitly religious orientation in the case of a Roman Catholic priest, however.) Nevertheless, this point of view shed light on certain dimensions of Pedro's and Sonia's situation that became a significant aspect of our common agenda. These included:

- o the place and function of their religious faith and its role in shaping their sense of personal identity (especially including issues of manhood and womanhood, the body and sexuality) and their relationship as a couple;
- o their images of and relationship with God, and the meaning and value of their intermittent participation in worship and other church practices;
- o their views of guilt, sin, and forgiveness in light of the Catholic teachings on love and human sexuality, and their actual sense of moral integrity and responsibility;
- o the possibility of growing morally and spiritually by seeking guidance for wise living.

Pastoral counseling goals. In this counseling situation I sought to maintain a balance between attention to the objectives pertaining separately to Pedro and to Sonia, and to the common objectives they owned as a couple seemingly in love with each other. Hence, our work together was oriented toward:

- facing their confusion, anxieties and fears, and feelings of shame and guilt, in ways that would bring relief and a sense of health and wholeness;
- gaining knowledge and understanding about human sexuality holistically, so that they could make better-informed decisions about becoming sexually active as a couple;
- clarifying the (Roman Catholic) church teachings about human sexuality and related questions of love, sin, prudence, responsibility, and emotional maturity, and their practical implications;
- evaluating their special relationship, with particular attention to certain family, sociocultural, and religious considerations, and planning possible next steps.

Counseling Pedro and Sonia presented a clear situation in which I needed to relate to them primarily as a moral guide,[10] contributing a blend of educative caregiving and pastoral counseling on ethical, value, and meaning issues.[11] Therefore, from my perspective as a pastoral counselor, I formulated and kept in mind several objectives for my work:

- to be a listening, supportive, and resourceful pastoral presence to Pedro and Sonia for the duration of the brief pastoral counseling process;
- to provide specific orientation regarding human sexuality, including understanding of pregnancy and contraception, in their larger life context of family, study and work, and faith;
- to make available to Pedro and Sonia diverse resources of the Christian faith in order to help them learn a process of discernment that might lead to wise choices as individuals and as a couple;

---

[10] The best available book on moral guidance as a crucial dimension of the ministry of pastoral care is Rebekah L. Miles, *The Pastor As Moral Guide* (Minneapolis: Fortress Press, 1999).

[11] Here I deliberately use the characterizations of *counseling on ethical, value, and meaning issues* and *educative counseling* in Clinebell, *Basic Types of Pastoral Care and Counseling,* chapters 6 and 13.

☐ to foster their emotional, moral, and spiritual growth, and to encourage them to seek support and guidance beyond the pastoral counseling setting.

With the discussion of these four pastoral counseling cases as the backdrop for further reflection, we can now proceed to address the fundamental, yet simple question: when (or how) is counseling *pastoral*? Alternatively, we ask: what makes pastoral counseling the kind of *counseling* that is pastoral? An initial response appears in the next section. I present a comprehensive answer to the question in chapters three and four.

AN EMERGING VISION FOR PASTORAL COUNSELING

The examination of different pastoral counseling situations as windows on the practice and experience of this special form of the ministry of pastoral care has illuminated key features of the vision of pastoral counseling I present in this book. The following three interconnected guidelines, growing out of the discussion so far, outline my view on the nature of pastoral counseling and its identifying characteristics.

First, in pastoral counseling it is essential to evaluate the counselees' situation four-dimensionally, as proposed by Loder. That is, we must not only consider transactions between self and world, the limited horizon normally considered in counseling and psychotherapy,[12] but also the larger framework of the threat of nonbeing—the void—and the possibility and invitation to new being—the Holy. Further, we must view and use the actual setting

---

[12] Naturally, I exclude from this generalization counseling and psychotherapy that intentionally includes spirituality issues and practices in a nonreductionist manner. See P. Scott Richards and Allen E. Bergin, *A Spiritual Strategy for Counseling and Psychotherapy* (Washington, D.C.: American Psychological Association, 1997); and William R. Miller, ed., *Integrating Spirituality into Treatment: Resources for Practitioners* (Washington, D.C.: American Psychological Association, 1999). These contributions include helpful material for considering spirituality both as subject matter in its own right (e.g., issues of acceptance, forgiveness, and hope,) and as resource for therapeutic intervention (e.g., meditation, prayer). For explicitly Christian perspectives, see the thirty-volume Resources for Christian Counseling series, ed. Gary R. Collins (Dallas: Word Publishing, 1991); and Mark R. McMinn, *Psychology, Theology, and Spirituality in Christian Counseling* (Wheaton: Tyndale House Publishers, 1996).

and process of pastoral counseling as a Christian ministry of care within these four dimensions as well (for example, by concretely honoring the partnership with the Spirit in our endeavors). Hence, philosophically speaking, pastoral counseling requires that we have clarity about three enduring fundamental issues: an adequate view of reality and being (metaphysics, ontology), a deep understanding of the nature of knowing and truth (epistemology), and a normative vision of the good life (personal and social ethics), as suggested in the next paragraph.

Second, it is indispensable to identify the pertinent issues of the counseling agenda from a psychological and a theological perspective, even as we work with an integrated understanding of those seeking care and of the setting and process of pastoral counseling. In other words, we must affirm the integrity of the disciplines of psychology and theology. As a means to this, we must avoid reducing either of them to the terms of the other, even as we maximize the potential for complementarity between their unique contributions. In any event, we must give priority to the theological and pastoral nature of our task, including reflection on the practice of pastoral counseling itself. This priority is worth emphasizing because of the ways theology addresses fundamental questions of life and thus distinctly informs the normative dimensions of pastoral counseling. What does it mean to live well in the light of God's reign and wisdom in the midst of our life's challenges and struggles? What is the shape of human completion and wholeness? How do we understand and foster maturity, and how do we know which is the way forward in human emergence?[13] These are questions theology is uniquely suited to address. By helping people make choices oriented to a more wholesome life, pastoral counseling fosters moral and spiritual growth in wise living.

Third, while recognizing the directive nature of pastoral counseling as a special form of the Christian ministry of care, it is also necessary to have clarity about the difference, the

---

[13] These are questions explicitly addressed by, among others, James W. Fowler, in *Becoming Adult, Becoming Christian: Human Development and Christian Faith,* rev. ed. (San Francisco: Jossey-Bass, 2000), and James E. Loder, *The Logic of the Spirit: Human Development in Theological Perspective* (San Francisco: Jossey-Bass, 1998).

complementarity, and the correlation between two distinct sets of pastoral counseling goals. On the one hand, goals must be selected and articulated from the perspective of those seeking care in consultation with pastoral caregivers, as they emerge from the former's felt needs for counseling. On the other hand, pastoral counselors must seek clarity also about goals that directly apply to their work as they seek to guide the counseling process. More importantly, pastoral counselors must honor the call they have received to mediate divine grace and wisdom as representatives of the caring church and the healing Christ. They must become competent caring people[14] whose character reflects their participation in faith communities fully attuned to the reign of God in the world[15] and who are committed to work as moral and spiritual guides.[16] In fact, these personal characteristics regarding call, competence, character, and commitment, together with the question of explicit accountability to the church in some formal way, are essential to define counseling that is pastoral.

What makes pastoral counseling *pastoral* as well as *counseling?* Further reflection on the four cases I presented above can shed light on this question. These cases again serve as backdrop as we focus on two common characteristics of pastoral counseling situations, perceived from the perspective of the counselor as pastoral caregiver. I will then conclude the chapter

---

[14] See, for example, the characterization of the caregiver as person, learner, and teacher, in John Patton, *Pastoral Care in Context: An Introduction to Pastoral Care,* (Louisville: Westminster John Knox Press, 1993), chapters 3 and 4.

[15] For an illuminating treatment of the relationship between the reign of God as an ethical culture, the church as an ethical community, and the therapist as an ethical character, see Alvin C. Dueck, *Between Jerusalem and Athens: Ethical Perspectives on Culture, Religion, and Psychotherapy* (Grand Rapids: Baker Books, 1995).

[16] Rebekah L. Miles notes that good guides have distinctive knowledge and wisdom and as practical pilgrims are constantly training and preparing themselves for their art. Further, good guides are confident leaders who know their limits and temptations, know when they need help and are willing to seek advice, remember that others are free and responsible, teach others the lessons of pilgrimage and guidance, and develop excellent capacities for discernment. They not only know the rules but also know that the rules must sometimes be bent or even changed, and remember the most important things—the shared destination and the source of power (*The Pastor As Moral Guide,* 6–7).

with a consideration of pastoral counseling as a way of doing practical theology.

OVERALL PURPOSE AND FUNDAMENTAL APPROACH: PASTORAL COUNSELING AND WISDOM IN THE LIGHT OF GOD

The four cases illustrate clearly that each pastoral counseling situation calls for specific goals, however we may articulate them. Each situation also requires the selection of pertinent strategies to reach these objectives. At the same time, it is also apparent that all pastoral counseling situations have much in common. While I searched for an alternative to mental health as the master metaphor for pastoral counseling,[17] my practice and research during the last several years led me to appreciate anew two basic commonalities of all pastoral counseling settings. These commonalities, I believe, point to wisdom in the light of God as a fitting alternative to the mental health metaphor.[18] These commonalities center on issues of overall purpose and fundamental process; consideration of these is necessary as we begin to characterize pastoral counseling as a unique form of Christian ministry.

A common purpose. Calvin, Kathy, Judy and Robert, and Pedro and Sonia had entered pastoral counseling relationships because they were experiencing disorientation in different forms and distress of varying degrees. In the course of our short-term counseling experiences, they were invited, implicitly rather than explicitly, to become wiser people in the light of God as we

---

[17] Mental health is the master metaphor for pastoral counseling according to the medical/psychiatric view and practice of pastoral counseling.

[18] Undoubtedly, pastoral counselors must be able to recognize indicators of psychopathology; further, they must be able to make timely referrals, as necessary, to competent mental health professionals. However, pastoral counselors should not be concerned *primarily* with restoring or enhancing mental health as defined in clinical psychology and psychiatry. Rather, as providers of a special form of pastoral care, pastoral counselors are primarily concerned with helping people live more wisely in the light of God as they face the kinds of life challenges and struggles illustrated in the cases presented above. In any event, our four-dimensional understanding of wisdom does not necessarily correlate with two-dimensional notions of mental health, however defined. In the remainder of the book, I systematically develop a constructive argument for adopting *wisdom in the light of God* as the master metaphor of pastoral counseling.

worked together in the face of the challenges and struggles they were encountering at that particular juncture of their life journeys. In each case, the overarching goal of becoming wiser included three inseparable aspects of the counselees' search for relief and resolution. As pastoral counselor, I needed to recognize that each of these aspects integrate psychological and spiritual perspectives on the self.

First, the counseling experience helped the counselees find newer and better ways of knowing and understanding reality multidimensionally, including the dimensions of self; social world; the threatening void; and the gracious, embracing Holy. From a Christian formation viewpoint, the counselees needed to grow in their ways of seeing, to increasingly perceive reality with the eyes of the living Parent God. Such growth in *vision* entailed the practice and development of a number of dispositions and behaviors, including attending; admiring and contemplating; and engaging in critical thinking, creative imagining, and spiritual discerning.

Second, the counseling experience encouraged the counselees to discover more fulfilling and faithful ways of being and loving, with specific attention to their relationships with others, with God, and with self. In Christian formation terms, their hearts needed to become increasingly conformed to the heart of Christ. Such growth in *virtue* entailed an ongoing process of formation and transformation shaping their inmost affections and passions, dispositions and attitudes—habits of the heart—and defining the content of their moral and spiritual character. In short, God was calling them to become unique expressions of divine love.

Third, the counseling experience empowered the counselees to make sound choices and to invest fresh energies in relationships, work, leisure, worship, and service, and to find ways to sustain those choices with integrity. They needed to find a freer and more hopeful orientation toward life in the midst of their particular social situations. Such growth in *vocation* may be viewed as participating increasingly in the life of the Spirit in the world. For the counselees it opened the possibility of a fruitful and joyful response to the invitation to partner with God in creative, liberating, sustaining, and renewing purpose and activity. As their ways of being and living became increasingly consistent with a wisdom understanding of divine purpose and activity, I anticipated that their lives would receive the gifts of further meaning, value, hope, and courage.

In summary, the common overall purpose of pastoral counseling was to help Calvin, Kathy, Judy and Robert, and Pedro and Sonia know how to live more hopeful, moral, and wholesome lives. In order to realize its potential as a ministry of care, pastoral counseling would need to awaken, nurture, and empower their moral and spiritual intelligence.[19] Indeed, these four cases suggest that pastoral counseling means to be transformative: its overall purpose includes but goes beyond emotional intelligence, which is commonly a goal of counseling and psychotherapy.[20] *Spiritual intelligence*, understood as wisdom in the light of God, transforms the emotional and other forms of intelligence; this occurs whenever the latter merely promote the adaptive or conforming aims and means of conventional and pragmatic wisdom in a given social and cultural milieu.

An overall approach. Each of these four cases demonstrates the importance of selecting diverse appropriate counseling strategies. Nevertheless, our collaborative work in all cases involved the

---

[19] The notion of *moral intelligence* is sometimes used as a present-day equivalent to *practical wisdom* (*phronesis*, in Greek, which in Aristotle's ethical writings meant the intelligence or wisdom of the good person, closely associated with virtue and good character). That term, or an equivalent, has become operational in moral education and in the teaching of virtues in particular. For a recent practical illustration, see Michele Borba, *Building Moral Intelligence: The Seven Essential Virtues That Teach Kids to Do the Right Thing* (San Francisco: Jossey-Bass, 2001). Borba highlights the seven virtues of conscience, empathy, self-control, respect, kindness, tolerance, and fairness. My use of moral intelligence includes a holistic consideration of virtue and character in spiritually grounded and theologically defined moral formation. Further, I use the term *spiritual intelligence* specifically in reference to *wisdom in the light of God*, which necessarily includes and transforms moral intelligence, as I explain in the following chapter.

[20] Popularized by Daniel Goleman's best seller, *Emotional Intelligence* (New York: Bantam, 1995), what is nowadays called emotional intelligence has always been a key focus of counseling and psychotherapy because its hallmarks are abilities such as self-awareness, empathy, management of feelings, motivation, and social skill. See also Reuven Bar-on and James D. A. Parker, eds., *The Handbook of Emotional Intelligence: Theory, Development, Assessment, and Application at Home, School, and in the Workplace* (San Francisco: Jossey-Bass, 2001).

pivotal practice of discernment as an essential aspect of pastoral counseling. Viewed from my perspective as pastoral counselor and theologian, in each of those four situations a multi-way, critical conversation took place. The conversation included the counselees' personal stories and hopes located in family and sociocultural contexts; human science viewpoints, insights and tools (especially from personality theory and developmental psychology, psychodynamic and cognitive therapy, and narrative and family systems theory); and theological, spiritual, and pastoral resources.[21] Stated in other terms, a hermeneutical activity led us to discern, first of all, what the particular situation called for; second, we needed to search for alternatives and to develop a course of action; and we also had to evaluate ongoing responses to the challenges and struggles the counselees faced.

From a theological perspective, the setting and the process of pastoral counseling encompassed more than counselors and psychotherapists usually recognize, at least explicitly. The four-dimensional understanding of reality, and of knowing, in particular, determined the nature of the overall approach and the discerning activity under discussion here. *Counseling* that was *pastoral* occurred not only in a safe therapeutic space but also in a *sacred* place where the presence and activity of the Spirit of God was also acknowledged (by at least the pastoral counselor). Further, we assumed partnership and collaboration with the Spirit in the process of counselees and counselor seeking to know the specific nature of the problems and the best ways to creatively confront and transform them.

Therefore, the activity of discernment, comprehensively viewed, conditioned the process (the *how*, or methods and techniques) as well as the content (the *what*, or themes and issues)

---

[21] To say that a *critical* conversation occurred means that the resources of the human sciences and theology, together with my personal and professional experience and expertise, were also subject to evaluation, correction, and improvement, even as they illuminated the counselees' life challenges and struggles and suggested ways to resolve them satisfactorily and wisely. In other words, the uniquely hermeneutical work characterizing the process of pastoral counseling that took place in the four cases must be viewed dialectically. The implication, in this light, is that pastoral counseling must always be practiced as a dialectical-hermeneutical process.

of pastoral counseling in significant ways. Further, learning the specific practice of discernment, especially as a collaborative, dialogical, and even prayerful endeavor, became a specific and overarching objective, an expected outcome for the counselees in all four cases. Indeed, an indicator of progress for Calvin, Kathy, Judy and Robert, and Pedro and Sonia, was their willingness and ability to engage in discernment. In other words, growth in wisdom entailed for them discerning and choosing wisely, as well as learning to act and behave wisely in a consistent fashion. *Wisdom in the light of God* supplied the guiding principle and the master metaphor of pastoral counseling because, as I present systematically in the next chapter, the way of wisdom thus understood and appropriated is about a process of knowing how to live a better life in the midst of our social and existential circumstances.

This brief discussion of the two commonalities of purpose and process in pastoral counseling suggests that this special form of the ministry of care is oriented by a certain vision of human emergence and flourishing. I therefore assume that pastoral caregivers and theologians will articulate an appropriate philosophy so that they may work with a sound personal and social ethic and a holistic epistemology. They must view their practice of care and their reflection on pastoral care, not only as an expression of Christian ministry in a specialized sense, but also as a potentially creative work of practical theology.

PASTORAL COUNSELING AS PRACTICAL THEOLOGY

There is a fundamental analogy between pastoral counseling (and pastoral theology as theological reflection on the ministry of care) and the structure of the discipline of practical theology understood as a theory of action. On the one hand, this analogy helps us recognize the similarities and the continuities between pastoral counseling and other arts of ministry such as teaching, mentoring, and spiritual guidance. On the other hand, the analogy helps us appreciate the uniqueness of pastoral counseling as a ministry practice, and pastoral theology as a critical and constructive reflection on that practice.

According to Gerben Heitink's helpful conceptualization, practical theology is a particular theory of action that involves hermeneutical, empirical, and strategic dimensions.[22] Similarly, in all pastoral counseling situations we must respond with interrelated perspectives of understanding, explanation, and orientation to choice and action. Obviously, our interest is not only to describe, interpret, and explain the expressions of human reality presented in all sorts of counseling situations but also to help people make wise choices and change toward healing and wholeness. Heitink defines the unique character of practical-theological method with reference to three interconnected circles in a circulation system of theory formation. In his words, "The three circles correspond to the distinctive goals of the discipline: the interpretation of human action in the light of the Christian tradition (the hermeneutical perspective), the analysis of human action with regard to its factuality and potentiality (the empirical perspective), and the development of action models and action strategies for the various domains of action (the strategic perspective)."[23] Pastoral care—traditionally included in the broader area of *poimenics*—is one of the action domains Heitink alludes to in which the overall structural model for viewing and doing practical theology can be applied.

Theory building in pastoral counseling and pastoral theology. One of the best examples of creative work in pastoral theology and pastoral counseling as a way of doing practical theology is Christie Cozad Neuger's recent contribution to the field. She has developed a liberationist pastoral theological method and a pastoral counseling model based on narrative counseling theory from a feminist perspective and commitment.[24] According to

---

[22] See Gerben Heitink, *Practical Theology: History, Theory, Action Domains*, trans. Reinder Bruinsma (Grand Rapids: Eerdmans, 1999). In this erudite book, Heitink formulates a comprehensive theory of practical theology, which he defines as "the empirically oriented theological theory of the mediation of the Christian faith in the praxis of modern society" (6).

[23] Ibid., 165.

[24] Christie Cozad Neuger, *Counseling Women: A Narrative, Pastoral Approach* (Minneapolis: Fortress Press, 2001). Neuger's original proposal for a new vision was presented in the essay, "Feminist Pastoral Theology and Pastoral Counseling: A Work in Process," *Journal of Pastoral Theology* 2 (summer 1992): 35–57. For a summary of her pastoral counseling model, see her essay, "Pastoral Counseling As an Art of Personal and Political Activism," in *The Arts of Ministry:*

Neuger's proposal, the goal of pastoral counseling is not just personal transformation but also transformation of the culture—including the church—as part of a larger transformational project through pastoral care. One may clearly visualize the three intersecting circles that define the task of practical theology in her mutually illuminating descriptions of the pastoral theological method, on the one hand, and the pastoral counseling model, on the other hand. A correlation methodology characterizes this way of doing practical theology. In Neuger's words, "Using the tool of empathic engagement, we engage in the methodological spiral that begins in the human story (in which the divine story is also partially embedded), moves to engage theological and other traditions, engages in reconstruction, and, out of practical wisdom and judgment, generates practices and performance of practices that are then brought to the particular story. The creative engagement of that encounter raises new questions and the spiral begins again. This becomes a practice of theology."[25] In this endeavor, it is crucial to determine whether those care and counseling practices offer liberating, empowering, and healing direction for those seeking care.

Directly related to Neuger's pastoral theological method is her four-phase feminist pastoral counseling framework and model for the practice of pastoral care in a counseling form. First, pastoral counseling begins with helping women come to voice, in a world in which women's voices are consistently silenced, discouraged, denied, and controlled. Second comes the task of helping women gain clarity, especially through reframing and restorying as means of resistance and transformation. Third, pastoral counseling helps women make choices for which they can claim relevance and accountability. Finally comes the task of help for staying connected, as an active and dynamic process of connection and relationality that is necessary for the maintenance

---

Feminist and Womanist Approaches, ed. Christie Cozad Neuger (Louisville: Westminster John Knox Press, 1996), 88–117. While Neuger's book focuses on pastoral counseling with women, including comprehensive consideration of three contexts of pastoral care—intimate violence, depression, and aging—its contribution illuminates the field broadly in both theory and practice.

[25] Neuger, *Counseling Women*, 229.

of counterstories and for the ongoing work of resistance to and transformation of oppressive and dominant forces.[26]

My proposal for pastoral counseling similarly stems from an understanding of practical theology as a theory of action involving hermeneutical, empirical, and strategic dimensions. This understanding was implicit in my presentation of the four cases in the first part of this chapter. In addition, I view pastoral counseling in the broader framework of pastoral care and Christian ministry contextually practiced in the service of human wholeness in the light of God. However, the proposal I present in this book has a specific theoretical focus: to reconsider pastoral counseling in terms of wisdom as the ground metaphor. Therefore, I will continue to orient my constructive work of practical and pastoral theology toward developing my thesis about the normative biblical-theological base of pastoral counseling. With that task in mind, I now turn to discuss why we must reclaim wisdom as the heart of pastoral counseling.

---

[26] Ibid., 230–2.

2 | Reclaiming wisdom as the heart

But where is wisdom to be found? (Job 28:12)

The fear of the Lord is the beginning of wisdom;
. . . the tongue of the wise brings healing. (Prov. 1:7a; 12:18b)

THESE WORDS OF OLD TESTAMENT WISDOM REMAIN AS FRESH
and pertinent as ever. For that reason I present a biblical and
theological rationale for reclaiming wisdom as the heart of
pastoral counseling as a ministry of the church.[1] The opening
section of this chapter explicitly connects two foundational
biblical motifs: the reign of God and wisdom in the light of God.
The discussion continues with a survey of wisdom in the biblical
tradition and in New Testament–based convictions about Jesus
and the wisdom of God. The subsequent section on understanding
and appropriating wisdom summarizes what I mean by the term
wisdom from a practical theological perspective. The final section
of the chapter then considers implications of my proposed understanding of wisdom for pastoral counseling.

THE REIGN OF GOD
AND WISDOM IN THE LIGHT OF GOD

For the last several years, my constructive reflection in the
discipline of practical theology has focused on the biblical symbol
of the reign of God in an ecclesiological frame of reference. I have
affirmed the church as the primary context for formation and

---

[1] Of course, I also assume that diverse kinds of human science foundations,
especially those stemming from psychology and psychotherapy, are also
essential for effective practice (including critical reflection on the counseling
practice as such). Further, there are diverse ways of articulating biblical and
theological foundations for pastoral care and counseling, as represented in the
selected bibliography. Two books that specifically focus on them are Leroy T.
Howe, *The Image of God: A Theology for Pastoral Care and Counseling* (Nashville:
Abingdon Press, 1995); and Howard W. Stone, *Theological Context for Pastoral
Caregiving: Word in Deed* (New York: Haworth Pastoral Press, 1996).

transformation, learning and human emergence, and for communal and societal change in the direction of the ethics and politics of God.[2] I am convinced that the horizon opened for us by the vision of God's commonwealth of freedom, justice, and peace, with all its ethical, political, and eschatological import, is indeed essential. Further, I hold that we must integrate this vision with a creative appropriation of wisdom in biblical and theological perspective.

The synoptic Gospels remind us that the reign of God is the key to understanding Jesus' life and ministry as a sage and teacher of divine wisdom. The symbol of God's reign evokes the tension between the *already*—gifts bestowed and divine dreams partially realized, as human dreams are transformed and realized in history—and the *not yet* of God's reign—divine promises and expectations for humankind and for the whole world, which intersect with our human longings. More specifically in terms of our interests, the reign of God also helps us challenge prevailing educational and psychological practices that foster domestication and adjustment to the dominant cultures in conformity with the conventional and pragmatic wisdoms of our times.

As I have sought to understand the symbol of the reign of God and to translate that understanding into operational guidelines for ministry, I have found that the biblical notion of wisdom provides a significant and useful epistemological key. Put

---

[2] In the area of educational ministry, see my book, *Religious Education Encounters Liberation Theology* (Birmingham: Religious Education Press, 1988); also my essays, "Liberation Theology and Religious Education," in *Theologies of Religious Education*, ed. Randolph C. Miller (Birmingham: Religious Education Press, 1995), 286–313; and "Education for Social Transformation," in *Mapping Christian Education: Approaches to Congregational Learning*, ed. Jack L. Seymour (Louisville: Abingdon Press, 1997), 23–40. In the area of theological education, see "The Church and Its Theological Education: A Vision," in *Theological Education on Five Continents: Anabaptist Perspectives*, ed. Nancy R. Heisey and Daniel S. Schipani (Strasbourg: Mennonite World Conference, 1997), 5–35; "The Three Contexts of Practical Theology: A Latin American Perspective with Implications for Theological Education," in *Globalisation and Difference*, ed. Paul Ballard and Pamela Couture (Cardiff: Cardiff University Press, 1999), 163–8. In the area of pastoral psychology and counseling, see "Bases eclesiológicas: La Iglesia como Comunidad Sanadora," in *Psicología y Consejo Pastoral: Perspectivas Hispanas*, ed. Daniel S. Schipani and Pablo A. Jiménez (Atlanta: Libros AETH, 1997), 3–25.

simply, we may view the reign of God as the ultimate normative culture in which God's dream for the world is being realized and will be fully realized beyond history. The notion of wisdom in the light of God in turn illuminates fundamental existential questions. How shall we live in conformity with that normative culture? And how shall we fashion together the kind of world that pleases God? Later in the chapter, I will suggest that Jesus Christ is the connection, both hermeneutically and existentially, between these two foundational biblical motifs—the reign of God and wisdom in the light of God.

Strictly speaking, the expression *wisdom in the light of God* does not appear in the Bible, although there are more than two hundred references to *wisdom* and a handful of references to *wisdom of God* in the New Revised Standard Version. I use the phrase to mean *wisdom that is in tune with, as well as dependent on, divine will (or wisdom)*. The phrase implies that we are able to recognize the historical and cultural reality of a variety of wisdoms. Thus, we acknowledge that there are lesser wisdoms (human prudence) as well as adversarial, alternative wisdoms (as implied, for instance, in 1 Corinthians 1:23, in reference to the wisdom that Paul calls "a stumbling block to Jews and foolishness to the Gentiles"). Further, the prevailing conventional and pragmatic wisdoms in any given culture are potentially, although not necessarily completely, in contradiction with wisdom in the light of God. In other words, just as we can speak of lesser or adversarial kingdoms in regard to the reign of God, we can also speak of lesser or alternative wisdoms in regard to wisdom in the light of God.[3] From this perspective, psychology itself may be viewed as playing the role of lesser or conventional wisdom in our western culture. This is clearly the case, given the function of psychology as major source of personal identity and provider of

---

[3] For example, in light of such a characterization, I hold that the dominant culture in the United States—so heavily determined by the economic structures, practices, and ideology of global market capitalism, on the one hand, and the militaristic and imperialistic nature of U.S. foreign policy, on the other hand—in many ways contradicts this understanding of both God's reign and divine wisdom.

ideology and technologies for the ordering and orientation of personal life and culture.[4]

Three reasons undergird my proposal to reclaim wisdom as the heart of pastoral counseling. First, wisdom, a significant part of the biblical tradition and of the Judeo-Christian theological heritage, represents a unique way of doing practical theology. Second, Jesus, the exemplar of caring in the light of divine grace, was a sage and teacher of wisdom; and Jesus, the Christ, is recognized as Savior and Lord and as God's Wisdom (Sophia) made flesh. Third, biblically grounded wisdom language and orientation are especially suitable when reappropriating pastoral counseling as a ministry of the church.

WISDOM IN THE BIBLICAL TRADITION

Although I am limited in my discussion of the topic by the brevity of this work, I will summarize here my understandings of wisdom in the biblical tradition as they have informed my reflection and practice. In the Hebrew and Near Eastern historical and cultural trajectory in which we are particularly interested, wisdom is a complex notion. It contains the following three interdependent meanings: (a) a movement, a sapiential tradition embodied in actual guidance, presumably carried out by actual sages; (b) a worldview and an approach to reality and manner of discernment that is both a way of knowing and a way of doing theology; and (c) a particular body of literature which documents (a) and (b) and serves as a reservoir of resources for further practical theological reflection and ministry practice. In other words, wisdom as a way of knowing and theologizing is mediated through a body of literature, much of which may have had its source in a sapiential tradition.[5]

---

[4] On this topic of the unique place and role of psychology in our culture, consider the complementary perspectives of Don S. Browning, *Religious Thought and the Modern Psychologies: A Critical Conversation on the Theology of Culture* (Philadelphia: Fortress Press, 1987); and Robert L. Woolfolk, *The Cure of Souls: Science, Values, and Psychotherapy* (San Francisco: Jossey-Bass, 1998).

[5] The following surveys on wisdom are especially helpful: Gerhard von Rad, *Wisdom in Israel* (Nashville: Abingdon Press, 1972); Kathleen M. O'Connor, *The Wisdom Literature* (Wilmington: Michael Glazier, 1988); Roland E. Murphy, *The Tree of Life: An Exploration of Biblical Wisdom Literature* (New York: Doubleday,

The search for wisdom is common to all cultures in the ancient Orient and the Near East in particular (especially Egypt and Mesopotamia). Further, Alexander's conquests in the fourth century B.C.E. ensured the widespread influence of Hellenistic culture in the region, including its notions and ways of wisdom. Israel had a share in this international and intercultural heritage. In any event, beyond the international commonalities, scholars generally recognize unique aspects of the Israelite wisdom documented in the Hebrew Bible. I highlight three of these. (a) Hebrew wisdom makes the extraordinary claim that the fear of the Lord is indispensable for becoming wise and is the basic orientation of wisdom. In other words, Israel's God of creation, liberation, and covenant remains preeminent (even if the overall interest of this way of theologizing is understandably focused on this world); and human experience is viewed, interpreted, and oriented in light of the knowledge of God. (b) The prevailing wisdom motif of human wholeness connects with biblical piety (holiness) in the framework of Israel's covenant life. The wise person tends to be identified with the righteous, and the unwise, or fool, with the unjust (e.g., Proverbs, chapters 10–15). From the perspective of biblical wisdom, wholeness and holiness go hand in hand. (c) Hebrew wisdom is theologically interpreted experience—an alternative way of doing theology—that implicitly claims a normative revelatory function; therefore we may understand the sages as playing the role of mediators of Yahweh to Israel.[6]

By using Jeremiah 18:18 as a way of entry into the Old Testament canon, we may begin identifying characteristics of

---

1990); Ronald E. Clements, *Wisdom in Theology* (Grand Rapids: Eerdmans, 1992); Leo G. Perdue, Bernard B. Scott, and William J. Wiseman, eds., *In Search for Wisdom: Essays in Memory of John G. Gammie* (Louisville: Westminster John Knox Press, 1993); Leo G. Perdue, *Wisdom and Creation: The Theology of Wisdom Literature* (Nashville: Abingdon Press, 1994); James L. Crenshaw, *Old Testament Wisdom: An Introduction*, rev. ed. (Louisville: Westminster John Knox Press, 1998); and Anthony R. Ceresko, *Introduction to Old Testament Wisdom: A Spirituality for Liberation* (Maryknoll: Orbis Books, 1999).

[6] See Walter Brueggemann, *Theology of the Old Testament: Testimony, Dispute, Advocacy* (Minneapolis: Fortress Press, 1997), chapter 24, "The Sage As Mediator."

biblical wisdom, as suggested by Walter Brueggemann,[7] among others. Wisdom—referred to by words such as *hokmah*, *binah*, *tebuna*, and *sakal*—seems to have evolved during the span of biblical tradition. Originally, wisdom was often portrayed as a skill or craft (Exod. 31:6, 36:2, 8) or as cleverness (2 Sam. 14:2). Eventually the concept emerged as a practical wisdom of life that brings success, respect, and personal well-being. Wisdom writers assumed that wisdom normally comes from reflection on life experience (Job 12:12), but it may also be learned from one's tradition (Prov. 19:20) and from other wise people (Isa. 19:11).

After the beginning of the monarchy, a special class of wise men and women emerged who were dedicated to the study and communication of wisdom (2 Sam. 14:2). By the time of Jeremiah and Ezekiel (sixth century B.C.E.), they may have taken their place alongside the prophets and the priests as a major influence. These agents of wisdom appear to have been regularly and socially accepted as having authority to reflect on and guide daily life, particularly in connection with certain occasions. The family and clan, the school, the royal court, and occasionally, the public arena were presumably the main contexts and social locations for sapiential work. Thus we may view the sages as practical theologians who engaged in the tasks of guidance and reflection in order to connect the challenges and struggles of current human experience, in its natural and social context, to the faith tradition of Israel.[8] While the sages probably added a reflective dimension to the Hebrew notion of wisdom, this wisdom always kept its practical and life-oriented meaning. They understood the locus of wisdom to be the *leb*, the heart or core of the person (Eccles. 10:3).

---

[7] Walter Brueggemann, *The Creative Word: Canon As a Model for Biblical Education* (Philadelphia: Fortress Press, 1982). See especially chapters 1, 4, and 5.

[8] Illuminating discussions about the sages can be found in the following books: Leo G. Perdue and John G. Gamme, eds., *The Sage in Israel and in the Ancient Near East* (Winona Lake: Eisenbrauns, 1990); Joseph Blenkinsopp, *Sage, Priest, Prophet: Religion and Intellectual Leadership in Ancient Israel* (Louisville: Westminster John Knox Press, 1995); and Lester L. Grabbe, *Priests, Prophets, Diviners, and Sages: A Socio-Historical Study of Religious Specialists in Ancient Israel* (Valley Forge: Trinity Press International, 1995). These and other authors help us visualize and understand the role and the unique contributions of the Hebrew sages as wisdom teachers, counselors, and scribes.

As a result, they always viewed wisdom and becoming wise holistically and as grounded in history.

In the post-exilic period, the emphasis was on wisdom as an ethical response to God's revelation and law. Wisdom was a gift of God, but it brought responsibility to live according to its way (Job 28). Wise people did God's will, and they especially promoted compassion, justice, and peace (Proverbs 2). The beginning of wisdom for humankind was defined as reverent acknowledgement of and respect for God, manifested by faithfulness to the covenant (Job 28:28); further, it was expected that the promised Messiah would have God's spirit of wisdom (Isa. 11:2). Ronald E. Clements asserts that Israelite wisdom made its most meaningful and lasting contribution after the exile, because Israel was forced to make the transition from a nation-state to a diaspora scattered among many nations. Wisdom thus offered a new framework for dealing with the nature and meaning of the world—a framework that was not nationalistic, monarchic, or cultic. "[The] moral demands and dilemmas of life occupied the center-stage of the teachers of wisdom, making it a profoundly ethical body of education and leading to a characteristically sapiential idea of virtue."[9] Clements documents how wisdom became connected with health (or well-being) and healing, the path of the good life (piety, morality, and virtue), and key ideas such as the household as primary context for blessing, parental guidance, and work ethic. He highlights wisdom's twofold concern with personal moral integrity and inner life.

In late Old Testament times, wisdom came to be associated with divine revelation. Later still, in the intertestamental period, it was directly identified with the Torah, as evidenced in Sirach 24, and Wisdom of Solomon 7. Interestingly, at that point the way of wisdom was explicitly connected not only with the fear of the Lord and obedience, but with love of the Lord as well (Sir. 2:15–16); thus the key texts of Deuteronomy 10:12–13 and 30:6 were restated in sapiential language. Eventually, the confluence of the

---

[9] Clements, *Wisdom in Theology*, 37. Clements's basic argument is that, after the exile, wisdom was the key to the development of a comprehensive worldview, a universalistic ethic, and an integrated understanding of human needs, obligations, and spirituality.

Torah and wisdom traditions became foundational in the formation of both rabbinic Judaism and Christian thought. Joseph Blenkinsopp, who studied this phenomenon, explains that one can trace the course of law and wisdom "as two great rivers which eventually flow together and find their outlet in rabbinic writings and early Christian theology."[10] Walter Brueggemann emphasizes that the mutually conditioning convergence of Torah and wisdom eventuated in interpretive practices characterized as an ongoing, open-ended, never-completed process of continual reflection on and interpretation of old traditions in light of new experience. Brueggemann concludes, "The convergence of Torah and wisdom has prescribed for the Jewish and Christian enterprises, the two 'peoples of the book,' the inescapable, definitive, and unending work of exegesis, and the inevitable interface of tradition and experience. This crucial and identity-giving work of interpretation means that the work is never finished, that the work is necessarily conflictual, and that interpretation remains as unsettled as life itself."[11] Brueggemann's observation is a helpful reminder for practical and pastoral theologians, and indeed for those engaged in any of the ministry arts—such as teaching, preaching, and pastoral counseling—which are inherently hermeneutical in character.

On the one hand, all reflection on wisdom is concerned with life and with the formation of wise people. On the other hand, biblical wisdom as theologically interpreted human experience is not homogeneous in terms of overall outlook and mood. As John Goldingay explains, what Proverbs affirms, Job and Ecclesiastes agonize over; the mood of the former is confidence, whereas the mood of the latter is questioning. He adds that the key expression of that questioning is their concern with human suffering and death, which threaten to subvert the confidence of conventional wisdom.[12] For Robert Johnston, Ecclesiastes reflects on the

---

[10] Joseph Blenkinsopp, *Wisdom and Law in the Old Testament: The Ordering of Life in Israel and Early Judaism,* rev. ed. (Oxford: Oxford University Press, 1995), 151.

[11] Brueggemann, *Theology of the Old Testament,* 689–91.

[12] John Goldingay, "Wisdom on Death and Suffering," in *Understanding Wisdom: Sources, Science, and Society,* ed. Warren S. Brown (Philadelphia and London: Templeton Foundation Press, 2000), 121–34.

empirical evidence when life's order often proves disorderly, particularly when wisdom does not seem to make sense in the face of suffering and death. The writer of Ecclesiastes is acknowledging the fundamental paradoxes that life presents. Like the author of Job, he hears and responds to wisdom's dialectic call, and provides negative evaluations as well as positive judgments.[13] Whether the contrasting strains of biblical wisdom must be seen as canceling each other out[14] or held side by side in tension—as equally valid and reflective of the inherent paradox of human life in the fallen creation—is open to further debate among biblical scholars. From a practical theological perspective, affirming the contradictions and embracing the paradoxes named or implied in and among biblical sources of wisdom seems to be the better alternative. This preference is especially important as we reclaim wisdom as the heart of pastoral counseling in the ministry of the church.

Taken as a whole, the biblical wisdom tradition presents a distinctive way of doing theology, for it deals with the fundamental questions of human existence and destiny in the light of divine action and will, while focusing on everyday, mundane experience. Brueggemann summarizes six aspects of scholarly consensus regarding biblical wisdom. Biblical wisdom is (a) a theology reflecting on creation; (b) with lived experience as

---

[13] Robert K. Johnston, "It Takes Wisdom to Use Wisdom Wisely," in *Understanding Wisdom*, ed. Brown, 148–9.

[14] The position that the conflict within Israel's wisdom tradition is one of the major conflicts in the Hebrew Bible (and in the New Testament, and identifiable through Christian history) is clearly articulated by Marcus J. Borg in *Reading the Bible Again for the First Time: Taking the Bible Seriously but Not Literally* (San Francisco: Harper San Francisco, 2001), chapter 7, "Reading Israel's Wisdom Again." While recognizing truth in conventional wisdom as reflected in Proverbs, Borg is concerned with the performance-and-reward view of life to which it leads. The inescapable cruel corollary is: "If your life fails to work out, it must be because you have done something wrong; trouble is your fault." Victims of tragedy, oppression, or abuse may thus be considered responsible for their hardship and blamed for their predicament. According to this view, Job's friends/counselors are merely the voice of Israel's conventional wisdom that can only offer inadequate counsel in the face of tragedy (159–61, 176–9). I have included another reference to this important topic in the last section of this chapter.

its data, generally not overridden by imposed interpretive categories or constructs; (c) in which experience is viewed as having reliability, regularity, and coherence, (d) including an unaccommodating ethical dimension; (e) a natural theology that discloses to serious discernment something of the hidden character and underpinnings of all of reality; i.e., what is given as true arises in lived experience rightly (or wisely) discerned; (f) a natural theology that reveals and discloses the God who creates, orders, and sustains reality—the generous, demanding guarantor of a viable life-order that can be trusted and counted on, but not lightly violated.[15] This tradition offers guidance for wise living through both pedagogy and counsel. It defines wise people as those who daily seek the way of wisdom and walk in that way. As Jesus said at the conclusion of the Sermon on the Mount, the wise are those who hear and act on the words of wisdom, thus building their house on rock (Matt. 7:24). It is to the New Testament witness to Jesus that we now turn our attention.

JESUS AND THE WISDOM OF GOD

The Gospels portray Jesus as a teacher of wisdom and a sage guided by the vision of the reign of God. Scholars suggest that he would have been seen as a Jewish prophetic sage whose message and style reflected the confluence of Hebrew sapiential, prophetic, apocalyptic, and legal forms and ideas. They further suggest that Jesus contributed to the development of Jewish wisdom and charted a course that the community of his followers would pursue in further developing wisdom content and forms. The work of Ben Witherington on this matter is particularly useful. He argues that *sage* is heuristically the most appropriate and comprehensive term for describing Jesus, because "he either casts his teaching in a recognizable sapiential form (e.g., an aphorism, or beatitude, or riddle), or uses the prophetic adaptation of sapiential speech—the narrative *mashal*. . . . He speaks by various

---

[15] Brueggemann, *Theology of the Old Testament*, 680–1. He has developed Gerhard von Rad's view of wisdom as an alternative way of doing theology, with his own notion of Israel's *counter testimony*: "that in much of life, if Yahweh is to be spoken of meaningfully, it must be a Yahweh who is not direct and visible, but who in fact is hidden in the ongoing daily process of life" (Ibid., 335).

means of figurative language, thus choosing to address his audience using indirect speech."[16] Further, Witherington's work restates two notions associated with the liberationist or emancipatory import of Jesus' wisdom teaching and overall ministry: First, Jesus' special concern is with the common people, with the marginalized and oppressed in particular. Second, Jesus embraces the prophetic and apocalyptic traditions about reversal—counter-order to the status quo—by divine will or intervention. (A typical example of reversal is "Many who are first will be last, and the last will be first" [Mark 10:31].)

I claim that Jesus is the clue, both hermeneutically and existentially, to grasping the connection between the two foundational biblical motifs of God's reign and wisdom in the light of God. Jesus communicated God's alternative wisdom, with an ethic and a politics of compassion particularly reflective of divine grace. Jesus' ministry thus became subversive as well as transformative and recreative because he confronted the established conventional wisdoms of his time; he challenged values, attitudes, practices, and understandings of goodness and wellness, and transformed them.[17] This is also the view of theologian Peter Hodgson, who underscores a fundamental connection between the source and the substance of Jesus' ministry, that is, between the images of *sophia* (wisdom) and *basileia* (kingdom). Hodgson states that sophia names the constitutive power of the basileia. It is an eminently practical wisdom aimed at transforming established structures and authorities determined by the prevailing logic of domination and violence. God's wisdom points to a new kind of communal existence in which each person exists for the sake of the other, a community of mutuality, solidarity, and inclusive wholeness. "The Wisdom of God is the new logic . . . of grace and freedom by

---

[16] See Ben Witherington III, *Jesus the Sage: The Pilgrimage of Wisdom* (Minneapolis: Fortress Press, 1994), 159.

[17] I have found Marcus Borg's insights on this point persuasive; see *Jesus: A New Vision: Spirit, Culture, and the Life of Discipleship* (San Francisco: Harper & Row, 1987), especially chapter 6; also, *Meeting Jesus Again for the First Time: The Historical Jesus and the Heart of Contemporary Faith* (San Francisco: Harper San Francisco, 1994), chapters 4 and 5.

which the basileia overturns the oppressive logic of the world . . . [and Jesus is] the Word of God and the Spirit of God because he is the Wisdom of God, the incarnation of God's caring, truthful, communicative Sophia, who sets us free from the lying, foolishness, and boasting of this world."[18]

Jesus' style of ministry was consistent with the wisdom tradition, and specifically, with a biblically grounded wisdom in the light of God. The records of his approaches—particularly his use of parables, proverbs, aphorisms, and sayings, and the very way he engaged people—document his being a teacher of wisdom. Indeed, Jesus was capable of employing the forms of traditional wisdom to challenge the ways of conventional wisdom, for the sake of the reign of God. On this question of Jesus' use and transformation of the wisdom tradition, the contributions of Leo Perdue and Bernard Scott are particularly interesting. Perdue underscores the observation that Jesus' wisdom sayings are present in each of the canonical sources (Q, Mark, Matthew, Luke). He concludes that the substantive presence of wisdom sayings suggests that our earliest sources for the sayings of Jesus point to a teacher engaged in the creation and transmission of wisdom. Further, Perdue underscores that Jesus' teaching connects with and participates in Israel's critical wisdom (which exposes the limitations of conventional wisdom) while uniquely announcing and advancing the creation of a new order, namely, the reign of God.[19] Scott probes the hypothesis that Jesus' distinctive voice is recognized in the way he innovates in the common wisdom tradition by "playing in minor keys" (Scott's phrase)—such as the presiding symbol of the kingdom of God— and using wisdom images against themselves. He concludes that Jesus' innovation in the wisdom tradition is the discovery of an individual sage's voice that subverts the voice of commonality.

---

[18] Peter C. Hodgson, *God's Wisdom: Toward a Theology of Education* (Louisville: Westminster John Knox Press, 1999), 96–7, 99.

[19] Leo G. Perdue, "The Wisdom Sayings of Jesus," *Forum* 2, no. 3 (September 1986): 3–35. For the interdisciplinary perspective and insights of an education theorist, see Charles F. Melchert, *Wise Teaching: Biblical Wisdom and Educational Ministry* (Valley Forge: Trinity Press International, 1998), chapter 6, "Why Didn't Jesus Tell Bible Stories?"

Jesus' way of wisdom entails a counter-order—an alternative, subversive wisdom from below—not an order that supports the status quo or the values of the powerful and wealthy. For even as we can find striking similarities and parallels, both in form and in content, between the work of Ben Sira and the Jesus tradition, we can also appreciate fundamental differences. Ben Sira's proverbs preserved and propagated traditional wisdom. As a respected and learned member of the scribal class, Ben Sira's teaching did not pose a major threat or challenge to the status quo; Jesus' wisdom teaching challenged it. This point is clearly made by Anthony Ceresko who also highlights the contrasting social locations of Ben Sira and Jesus: for Jesus, the sage "from below," compassion represented the bottom line, the ultimate criterion in determining the way one should live. Jesus "demonstrates in a striking way the liberating potential of proverb and parable. . . . The strategy of Jesus in proposing his counter-order through story and wisdom sayings represents a strategy for liberation, a strategy for life, life with God in a just and life-giving community."[20] Finally, Witherington argues paradoxically that the source and inspiration of that counter-order "from below" was simultaneously "from above"; it was the in-breaking eschatological reign of God.[21]

Because, as I have suggested, Jesus models for us a unique pedagogical and pastoral approach for guidance in wise living, through an ethical, righteous way of life, these considerations regarding the source and the substance of his ministry are indispensable. Once again, we can creatively appropriate necessary foundational material for our work and reflection on pastoral care and counseling in particular. This is because Jesus' approach as portrayed in the four Gospels includes nurturing, reconciling, supporting, liberating, and healing dimensions. In other words, Jesus also models for us the stance of critical care in both the proximate and the ultimate goals of wise living. Such a stance focuses fundamentally on the primacy of love of God and neighbor as oneself.

We may take these convictions one step further: Jesus the Christ embodies the wisdom of God. According to New

---

[20] Ceresko, *Introduction to Old Testament Wisdom*, 171–5.

[21] Witherington, *Jesus the Sage*, 201.

Testament documentation, already the early followers of Jesus viewed him not only as an extraordinary sage but also as someone uniquely connected with divine wisdom and the very embodiment of that wisdom (Matt. 12:42 and Luke 11:31; Matt. 11:27; Luke 10:22; Matt. 11:19, 28–30; Luke 21:15, etc.). In his discussion of the formative influence of Old Testament temple traditions on the synoptic narratives, Willard Swartley emphasizes that Mathew deliberately identifies Jesus with wisdom. He asserts that "Jesus, by virtue of wisdom's function in Israel's traditions, is thus linked to both revelational and authoritative teaching (instructional) roles; by identifying Jesus with wisdom Matthew legitimates Jesus' Torah teaching and prophetic proclamation."[22] In Jesus, the personification of wisdom (Sophia) became definitively imagined and christologically conceptualized. There had been, of course, a long tradition of personification (for instance, in Proverbs wisdom is the giver of life [4:13] and the craftsperson whom God employs in the work of creation [8:30]). According to Roland Murphy, the personification of wisdom (Lady Wisdom) is an outstanding feature of biblical wisdom, and it is unique in the Bible, for both its quantity and its quality.[23] Other scholars suggest that the biblical tradition of wisdom/sophia was the culmination of the personification of God's presence and activity in Hebrew Scripture. Furthermore, the words, functions, and characteristics of sophia were eventually associated with the human being Jesus. In other words, sophia became Jesus the human being. Not only was the centrality of sophia language highlighted by the early Christian movement, but so was the gender complementarity of these Christologies, metaphorically speaking.[24] Marcus Borg summarizes his review of

---

22 Willard M. Swartley, *Israel's Scripture Traditions and the Synoptic Gospels: Story Shaping Story* (Peabody: Hendrickson Publishers, Inc., 1994), 181. For a more detailed and focused discussion of this topic, see Celia M. Deutsch, *Lady Wisdom, Jesus, and the Sages: Metaphor and Social Context in Matthew's Gospel* (Valley Forge: Trinity Press International, 1996), especially chapter 2, "Jesus As Wisdom: Matthew Transforms a Metaphor."

23 Roland E. Murphy, "Wisdom in the Old Testament," in *The Anchor Bible Dictionary*, ed. David N. Freeman (New York: Doubleday, 1992), 6:920–31.

24 See, for instance, Elizabeth Johnson, *She Who Is: The Mystery of God in Feminist Theological Discourse* (New York: Crossroad Publishing Company, 1993), 86–100;

the christological image of sophia in this way, "The use of sophia language to speak about Jesus goes back to the earliest layers of the developing [christological] tradition. . . . According to the Synoptics, Paul, and John, that which was present in Jesus was the Sophia of God."[25]

The relationship between Jesus as sage and Jesus as wisdom lies in part in his being the personal embodiment of his message; indeed, the New Testament documents, the church's teachings, and personal experience compel us to see Jesus himself as a living parable of God's life and wisdom. Hence, Denis Edwards argues that viewed "from below," Jesus is the human being whose own life and ministry profoundly embody the wisdom of God; viewed "from above," Jesus is the divine wisdom incarnate.[26] According to Peter Hodgson, what is distinctive about Jesus is the uniquely powerful manifestation of divine wisdom in his ministry, which integrates his teaching with his praxis of care, healing, and gathering. His teaching assumes a normative, paradigmatic quality in human history. Jesus reveals the true meaning of God and human life, and empowers human beings to discover the truth in their own circumstances and to engage in transformative practices: "a liberation or emancipation from whatever holds us in bondage (ignorance, superstition, idolatries, ideologies, anxieties, oppressive structures). We must engage in the work of emancipation ourselves; God in Christ empowers us to do so. . . . God's Wisdom engenders a paideutic process in human history."[27]

Further, we perceive Jesus not just announcing the in-breaking of God's reign but also believing that he was an active agent for its realization. The question of whether Jesus identified himself as the embodiment of wisdom with a transcendent self-understanding and consciousness, however, is subject to speculation and debate. Ben Witherington, for instance, believes

---

also Elisabeth Schüssler Fiorenza, *Jesus: Miriam's Child, Sophia's Prophet: Critical Issues in Feminist Christology* (New York: Continuum Publishing Company, 1994); and Denis Edwards, *Jesus the Wisdom of God: An Ecological Theology* (Maryknoll: Orbis Books, 1995).

[25] Borg, *Meeting Jesus Again for the First Time*, 109.

[26] Edwards, *Jesus the Wisdom of God*, chapter 2.

[27] Hodgson, *God's Wisdom*, 98, 103.

that to have been the case. Building on his research on the Christology of Jesus, he concludes that the early church took the seed of the unprecedented association by Jesus of a historical individual with God's personified wisdom, planted it and raised a vast harvest of wisdom Christologies, found in such varied contexts as Q, christological hymns, Paul, and the narrative framework of the Gospels. He then asks, rhetorically, "How better to explain the appearance of the idea of the historical person Jesus being identified or portrayed as Wisdom in so many different sources, many of which have no interconnections, than to assume that Jesus in some way presented himself as Wisdom?"[28] Be that as it may, the Gospels and the rest of the New Testament make clear that becoming a disciple of Jesus Christ includes the call and the spiritual empowerment to live wisely as Jesus of Nazareth lived. This living is according to the "wisdom from above ... which is pure and gentle, and full of the good fruits of kindness, mercy, righteousness and peace" (James 3:17–18).

INTERLUDE:
UNDERSTANDING AND APPROPRIATING WISDOM

Before I discuss some of the implications of focusing on wisdom in the light of God as the master metaphor for pastoral counseling, I want to describe what I mean by wisdom in the context of ministry practice and theological reflection. The following four paragraphs thus serve as a hinge between the first and last sections of the chapter.

First, it is possible to translate our common understandings of wisdom as character and behavior, including biblical under-standings, into present-day human science categories. For example, Warren Brown summarizes a number of recent contributions on the matter by combining several features highlighted in recent studies. In his perspective, wisdom may be viewed as emerging from (a) ready access to long-term memories of accumulated information and experience; (b) an ability to reason adequately based on that experience; (c) adequate ability to solve problems, particularly about social situations; (d) normal

---

[28] Witherington, *Jesus the Sage*, 208. See also Ben Witherington, *Christology of Jesus* (Minneapolis: Fortress Press, 1990), 263–75.

interactions between cognitive processing and the emotional responses that strongly influence our decisions; and (e) an ability to comprehend and use the cultural accumulation of wisdom typically represented in wisdom sayings and literature. (f) All these capacities converge to engender a new heuristic, a means for learning and adapting to our environment, which includes creative and transforming ways of doing so.[29] Brown acknowledges that this kind of operational understanding is necessarily reductionistic. Indeed, from a theological perspective, we need a larger framework, which, in addition to these views on wisdom, can help us grasp and work explicitly with three philosophical essentials. These three concepts, which are particularly necessary for the practice of and reflection on pastoral counseling, have to do with the nature of reality, the sources and nature of knowing, and the normative patterns of the good life.[30]

Second, wisdom is a complex and multilayered concept which includes not only the personal level but also social and cultural levels. Wisdom is a matter of behavior and character, recognizable as the knowledge and practice of living well (that is, of becoming an agent in right relationships and doing what is good for oneself and the community). Further, the sources of wisdom include resources that are both internal (e.g., commitment to learning, desire to grow, positive values, social competencies, positive identity and self-understanding) and external (e.g. support and encouragement, empowerment, boundaries and expectations, mentoring, guidance). Biblically grounded and theologically viewed notions of wisdom blend moral and spiritual

---

[29] Warren S. Brown, "A Scientific Study of Wisdom (Or Its Contributing Parts)," in *Understanding Wisdom*, ed. Brown, 307–15.

[30] As I discussed in the previous chapter, pastoral counselors must recognize that reality is not merely two-dimensional (i.e., simply a matter of self and environment/world) but four-dimensional. They must acknowledge the additional dimensions that are the possibilities of evil and not being, as well as new being, by God's grace and power. Further, they must realize that knowing deeply, in ways that foster guidance, discernment, reconciliation, support, liberation, and healing, requires attending to these four dimensions. It is in that light that pastoral counseling aims at awakening, nurturing, and developing people's moral and spiritual intelligence, i.e., living wisely—or how to live well—in the face of life's challenges and struggles.

dimensions by presenting wisdom and becoming wise as living in accordance with the knowledge and the love of God. Further, God's wisdom is acknowledged as the ultimate ground and goal of our human endeavors to sponsor wholeness and fullness of life. Therefore I propose that wisdom is the heart of pastoral counseling, which fundamentally calls for awakening, nurturing, and developing people's moral and spiritual intelligence. Pastoral counseling is a unique setting which offers the possibility of becoming wiser, an extraordinary setting where formation and transformation are expected to happen ultimately as a divine gift.

Third, on the personal level, the goal of becoming wiser in the light of God may be appreciated afresh in terms of the categories of seeing/knowing, valuing/being, and doing/living. Indeed, indicators of growth in wisdom—or becoming wiser in the light of God—may be identified in terms of the threefold pattern of the human spirit I have proposed, namely, vision, virtue, and vocation.[31] Interestingly enough, the very terms *wise* and *wisdom* connect etymologically with seeing and knowing.[32] Therefore, wisdom may be defined as "insightful seeing or visioning, an intellectual intuition or imaging through which something takes form (mental and/or visual) and a practice ensues."[33] Including but transcending the categories of the cognitive domain as commonly used, vision, theologically speaking, includes a number of aspects such as respectful attending, spiritual sensitivity and

---

[31] Descriptions of such a threefold pattern can be found in Daniel S. Schipani, *Comunicación con la juventud: Diseño para una nueva pastoral* (San Juan: Seminario Evangélico de Puerto Rico, 1994), chapters 1 and 2; and "Education for Social Transformation." A fuller discussion appears in an unpublished paper, "The Purpose of Ministry: Human Emergence in the Light of Jesus Christ," which will be part of another book project.

[32] In English, the words *wisdom* and *wise* derive from an Indo-European root, *weid-*, which means *to see* or *to know*. They are related to the Greek *eidos* (idea, form, seeing), to the Latin *videre* (to see), and to the modern German *wissen* (to know) (Hodgson, *God's Wisdom*, 88–9).

[33] Ibid., 89. I agree with Peter G. Hodgson that such an understanding of wisdom (*sophia*)—which includes apprehension and appreciation as well as critical reflection and an orientation to practice based on life experience—incorporates the Aristotelian notion of practical reason and knowledge with moral import and ends (*phronesis*) (ibid., 7).

perspective, critical awareness, creative imagination, and spiritual discernment. Vision, thus broadly understood, must be considered together with virtue (the formation and transformation of the heart) and vocation (participation in the life of God in the world and partnership with the Spirit).

Fourth, discernment is essential in the practice of wisdom. Becoming wiser always involves the disposition and the capacity to discern not only the better means to reach our life goals, but especially, which goals are truly worth valuing and seeking. More specifically, discerning the way of wisdom is essential when one is confronted with existential challenges (for example, needing to make key vocational decisions) and struggles (for instance, facing the death of a loved one). Discernment, including deliberation and judgment, is thus a key to both process and content in pastoral counseling, and it must be seen and guided as inseparable from the outcome(s) being sought (for example, making and implementing an important vocational decision, grieving in a wholesome way, healing). Put in the simplest terms, we behave wisely whenever we are able to discern what is the right thing to do, and act in such a way as to bring this about. In pastoral counseling, goals (counseling objectives, expected outcomes, or *what for*) must be considered together with discernment as key to the questions of process (counseling method, strategy, or *how*) and content (actual problem, agreed-on focus, or *what*). The main role of the pastoral counselor, fittingly enough, is to guide the process, for guidance and wisdom go hand in hand.[34]

WISDOM AND PASTORAL COUNSELING

In his substantial introduction to the field of pastoral care, Charles Gerkin reminds us that we must reclaim the three primordial Old Testament role models—prophets, priests, wise guides—to help us view, appreciate, and carry out the caring ministry of the Christian community and its leadership today. The prophets

---

[34] There is indeed an interesting connection between *wisdom* and *guidance* in light of etymological considerations. Rebekah L. Miles reports that the word *guide* comes from an ancient Romanic word, *widare*, which means *to know*. The words *wise, wisdom, wit*, and *guide* all share the same origin. *The Pastor As Moral Guide* (Minneapolis: Fortress Press, 1999), 4.

spoke for the tradition and its concern for response to the voice of God; the priests led the community in its cultic worship; the wise ones offered guidance to help the people in the daily affairs of individual and family life. Gerkin proposes in addition that the care of the people of God always involves three foci of concern that must be brought into three-way interactive tension. Gerkin states: "[Pastoral care] necessitates giving attention to ongoing care for the Christian tradition that grounds the faith and practice of the life of the people. It likewise involves attending to the life of the community of faith with care and discernment. In addition, it involves giving careful attention to the needs and problems of individuals and families.[35] While in this book I focus specifically on pastoral counseling, I assume—in agreement with Gerkin— that the larger arena of pastoral care calls for a more comprehensive consideration of sources, foundations, and practical guidelines. Further, I assume that the integrity and effectiveness of pastoral counseling, strictly speaking, depends in good measure on the supporting role of other aspects of caring. These aspects include the tradition that shapes Christian identity (the prophetic dimension), and the life and ministry of the faith community (the priestly dimension).

To connect the way of wisdom with the ministry art of pastoral counseling is fitting because of the historical background and continuity we can detect going back many centuries before the dawn of what we call counseling and psychotherapy. In fact, authors such as Thomas C. Oden argue convincingly that long before psychology was a distinct profession, pastors engaged in practices that necessitate what today we identify as psychological competence.[36] The biblical base and resonance of the notion of

---

[35] Charles V. Gerkin, *An Introduction to Pastoral Care* (Nashville: Abingdon Press, 1997), 26–7; especially chapters 1 and 3.

[36] For an illuminating presentation and discussion of classical pastoral wisdom, see the four-volume Classical Pastoral Care Series, edited by Thomas C. Oden (New York: Crossroad Publishing Company, 1986–1989). Oden presents and comments on texts drawn mainly from patristic, and to a lesser degree, medieval and Reformation sources that focus on soul care, the pastoral relationship, pastoral empathy, congruence, befriending, the timing of seasonable counsel, truth telling, admonition, and the role of Scripture in counseling. Consider especially *Pastoral Counsel* (1989). I first became interested in the biblical and

wisdom, and the soundness of the supporting historical, pastoral, and practical theological reflection justify the appropriation of wisdom as the master metaphor for pastoral counseling.[37] Some significant implications are highlighted below.

As I indicated earlier, biblical wisdom addresses fundamental existential questions. How shall we live in conformity with the normative culture of the reign of God? And how shall we together fashion the kind of world that pleases God? This wisdom connotes a holistic view of life and human behavior in the larger contexts of family and society, nature and the whole world. It is foundational for pastoral counselors because, as alternative wisdom, it supplies critical content in the face of conventional and lesser wisdoms, as well as constructive content in the manner of guidelines for wholesome living. Furthermore, the overall stance of wise counselors is not primarily that of trying to diagnose what is wrong with people and then figuring out how the human

---

historical foundations of pastoral counseling during my work on a doctoral thesis in psychology. At that point I established connections between wisdom in Israel and the practice of counseling, as documented in my first book, *La angustia y la dimension trascendente* [anxiety and the transcendent dimension] (Buenos Aires: La Aurora, 1969), 114–21.

[37] Don S. Browning has discussed the contemporary turn to practical philosophy as a way of understanding a new vision, and significant advances observable in the discipline of practical theology. See his book, *A Fundamental Practical Theology: Descriptive and Strategic Proposals* (Minneapolis: Fortress Press, 1991), especially chapter 2, "Exploring Practical Wisdom and Understanding." He focuses on the Aristotelian notion of *phronesis* as practical wisdom, with reference to the contribution of Hans-Georg Gadamer (who suggested that phronesis or practical wisdom may serve as a model of the process of understanding and interpretation, including a broadly moral concern for application). In light of our interests and agenda, Browning's contribution is significant, including, in that book, his reformulation of theology in terms of "fundamental practical theology" with four submovements (descriptive, historical, systematic, and strategic theology). His discussion of practical wisdom does not include an explicit consideration of biblically grounded views of wisdom. My view on this issue is that a redefined notion of phronesis (i.e., a lived-in-knowledge of the kind of world we should be fashioning together, a definition practical theologians have suggested) can help us better understand and articulate wisdom in the light of God. However, given the latter's biblical and historical base and theological and spiritual import, one should not simply replace it with phronesis in the sense originally intended by Aristotle and recently recovered by Gadamer and others.

sciences, notably psychology, determine the nature of the possible cure and the prescribed course of action and solution. The primary concern can be simply stated with the language of the psalmist's prayer, "So teach us to count our days that we may gain a wise heart" (Ps. 90:12), or with the counsel of the letter to the Ephesians, in the same key: "Be careful then how you live, not as unwise people but as wise, making the most of the time. . . . Understand what the will of the Lord is" (Eph. 5:15–17). The overall stance, therefore, is a hopeful and empowering approach inspired and sustained by divine grace in the face of any circumstance that would make special care in the form of counseling desirable or necessary. Rodney J. Hunter also states that, while modern pastoral care and counseling have tended to define their primary goals therapeutically, their goals should also be regarded as sapiential, the seeking of wisdom and the development of morally and spiritually profound forms of practical knowing, such as knowing how to love and how to suffer.[38]

By appropriating the foundation and frame of reference supplied by wisdom in the light of God, *we can better affirm the continuity and the complementarity that exist among diverse ministry arts*, especially teaching,[39] preaching, mentoring, youth ministry, and spiritual direction. In each of those ministry forms and settings, wisdom can be considered as both the way and the orientation. For example, Thomas H. Groome has proposed that wisdom similarly understood is the highest purpose of education

---

[38] Rodney J. Hunter, "Wisdom and Practical Knowledge in Pastoral Care," in *Dictionary of Pastoral Care and Counseling*, ed. Rodney J. Hunter (Nashville: Abingdon Press, 1990), 1325–6.

[39] In the case of educational ministry, Thomas H. Groome began to articulate a similar proposal with his use of the concept of *conation*, in *Sharing Faith: A Comprehensive Approach to Religious Education and Pastoral Ministry* (San Francisco: Harper San Francisco, 1991), 26–32. For a more recent redefinition, see Groome's "Religious Knowing: Still Looking for that Tree," *Religious Education* 92 (spring 1997): 204–26; and *Educating for Life: A Spiritual Vision for Every Teacher and Parent* (Allen, Tex.: Thomas More, 1999), 268–318. For a comprehensive treatment of wisdom from an interdisciplinary perspective involving biblical and educational studies, see Charles F. Melchert, *Wise Teaching*. For a Christian theology of education (as distinguished from a theology of Christian religious education), see Hodgson, *God's Wisdom*.

because it is holistic, engages the whole person, and encourages integrity and congruence between knowing and doing.[40] Indeed, the biblically grounded notion of wisdom supplies an appropriate way for us to state our intended goals of learning, formation, growth, and healing. These goals contribute to the overall purpose of ministry, which I define as *sponsoring human emergence in the light of Jesus Christ*. It is clear that a general purpose such as this calls for growth in wisdom; conversely, human emergence and growth in the life of the Christian faith make it possible and imperative to further grow in wisdom in the light of God. Because we understand pastoral counseling to be a ministry of the church, an explication of this definition of the purpose of ministry, at which pastoral counseling is thus supposed to aim, is in order:

First, *sponsoring* connotes the prevailing mode and style of Christian ministry according to the paradigm of Jesus recorded in the Gospels—a way of being and walking with others character- ized by compassionate initiative, hospitable inclusiveness, gentle empowerment, and a generous invitation to partnership and community; the term combines the senses of pointing to, encouraging, facilitating, guiding, and enabling.

Second, *human emergence* means a process of humanization viewed primarily in theological perspective. It is a reference to becoming more human through God's gift and promise of authentic freedom and wholeness. It connotes human becoming according to the wider ethico-political and eschatological framework of God's reign, the commonwealth of love, peace, and justice, and overall wellness. Hence, the process of emerging involves formation and transformation in the personal and communal life and faith journey that we commonly call spiritual and moral growth. I do not merely equate human emergence with psychological notions of development and maturation, although connections with natural human development and with psychological understandings must be adequately established and used in the practice and theory of Christian ministry, and of pastoral counseling in particular.

Third, the phrase *in the light of Jesus Christ* expresses a conviction that the wisdom of God as embodied in Jesus of

---

[40] Groome, *Educating for Life*, 278–98.

Nazareth determines the way and direction of authentic human emergence. This phrase also implies that such a norm is especially revealed in Scripture and that we can recognize it under the guidance of the gracious and illuminating Spirit of God. It further claims that we can reliably discern glimpses of human becoming in the light of Jesus Christ as historically (that is, particularly and concretely) manifested in the formation and transformation of individuals and communities by the power of the Spirit.

By proposing that pastoral counselors must perceive themselves primarily as caregiving sages, *wisdom also illuminates the question of what makes pastoral counseling truly pastoral.*[41] In the tradition of the sages we can recognize a number of desirable personal characteristics and benchmarks. Sages are attentive and admiring observers as well as empathic, realistic, and in touch with common humanity; they perceive human life in light of the wider ordering of the universe; they seek to bring culture to its proper expressions through the lives of people; they speak to those gray areas of human life where law is not explicit and which prophets do not directly address; they know that what is wise is life-enhancing ("those who find me find life" [Prov. 8:35; 3:18, 22]); they mediate what is and what ought to be. Further, sages are called to model values and ideals that include the following: the central place of good human relationships as life focus; the search for human emergence and growth in wisdom while recognizing actual limits; the fashioning of one's own humanity while recognizing the place of mystery over mastery; the affirmation of freedom, peace, joy, and hope, in lifestyles of grateful acceptance; the clarification of values and alternatives for the sake of wholesome discernment and choice, and so on. This is a picture consistent with one of the images of the pastoral caregiver proposed by Alastair Campbell, that of the wise fool.[42]

---

[41] Robert A. Coughenour explicates the notion of caregiving sage, in "The Role of the Sage As a Model for the Pastoral Counselor," notes from an undated and unpublished presentation to the American Association of Pastoral Counselors. I am indebted to Coughenour, dean and professor emeritus of Old Testament at Western Theological Seminary, for the following characterization of the sages.

[42] See Alastair V. Campbell, *Recovering Pastoral Care* (Philadelphia: Westminster Press, 1981), chapter 5. Campbell also proposes the images of pastoral caregiver as shepherd and wounded healer.

Therefore, I and others have suggested that *the correlation between the role of traditional sages and the role of pastoral counselors is significant.* For Robert J. Coughenour an explicit correlation (a) helps acknowledge the unique identity and vocation of the pastoral counselor; (b) helps the church better appreciate and benefit from the unique role of pastoral counselors in the larger ministry area of pastoral care; and (c) helps in the education of pastoral counselors both in formulating theoretical foundations— theological as well as psychological—and in structuring practical experiential components.[43] Another writer who directly relates the contributions of the biblical wisdom tradition to present day pastoral caregiving is Donald Capps, who proposes a therapeutic wisdom model that draws on the wisdom tradition and on the work of Erik Erikson. In that light, Capps has identified three pastoral roles—moral counselor, ritual coordinator, and personal comforter.[44]

On a more theoretical level, *the Judeo-Christian wisdom tradition provides a model for interdisciplinary conversation and collaboration.* This is so because the tradition includes both the way of doing theology we recognize as practical theology and a body of scriptural resources that has creatively appropriated materials from beyond the faith tradition. Indeed, biblical wisdom encourages the study of human nature, behavior, and change, by drawing from sources outside the canon of Scripture as well as in Scripture itself. Further, it invites us to engage in the tasks of empirical observation, reflective pondering, and application in a certain course of action.[45] Biblical wisdom suggests that it is possible to be a keen interpreter of the human predicament in this world while holding to a faith that provides an overarching frame of reference. Thus Gladson and Lucas propose that biblical wisdom presents a model for dialogue, "when understood as a

---

[43] Coughenour, notes and personal conversation.

[44] Donald Capps, *The Life Cycle Theory and Pastoral Care* (Philadelphia: Fortress Press, 1983), especially chapter 5. See also *Biblical Approaches to Pastoral Counseling* (Philadelphia: Westminster Press, 1981); and *Reframing: A New Method in Pastoral Care* (Minneapolis: Fortress Press, 1990).

[45] John W. Hilber, "Old Testament Wisdom and the Integration Debate in Christian Counseling," *Bibliotheca Sacra* 155 (October-December 1998): 411–22.

potential resolution to the epistemological impasse between psychology and religion."[46] From a theological perspective, C. Richard Wells suggests, given the peculiar relationship between wholeness and holiness in biblical wisdom, that wisdom provides an ideal context for reenvisioning our understanding of human wholeness in the framework of biblical theology.[47]

Finally, *it takes wisdom in the light of God to use wisdom wisely in pastoral counseling*. Lest we unduly idealize the sages of old, present-day pastoral counselors must also remain aware of the potential distortions and unfaithfulness detectable among Israel's sages. Three of those possible distortions are also threats and temptations for us today: (a) *settled traditionalism*, a lack of critical awareness which leads to mere cultural conformity; (b) *legalism*, closely related to traditionalism, in which old connections between deeds and consequences become frozen into absolutist principle in terms of pious wisdom; and (c) *compromising opportunism*, which suppresses the prophetic dimension by accommodation to the counselee's self-interest, or by tailoring counseling to the interest of the counselor.[48] Pastoral theologian Donald Capps has insightfully analyzed the inadequacy of the intervention of Job's friends/counselors, Eliphaz, Bildad, and Zophar. He identifies theological deficiencies in their approaches to Job's existential struggles, which roughly correlate with the commonly used methods of, respectively, supportive counseling; crisis counseling; and counseling on ethical, value, and meaning issues.[49] Capps uses a wisdom approach to the study of this wisdom text, which includes a detailed account of an attempt to apply wisdom to make sense of Job's condition while seeking to

---

[46] Jerry Gladson and Ron Lucas, "Hebrew Wisdom and Psychotheological Dialogue," *Zygon* 24 (September 1989): 357–76.

[47] C. Richard Wells, "Hebrew Wisdom As a Quest for Wholeness and Holiness," *Journal of Psychology and Christianity* 15 (1996): 58–69. For a complementary study with guidelines on biblical interpretation, see Richard Schultz, "Responsible Hermeneutics for Wisdom Literature," in *Care for the Soul: Exploring the Intersection of Psychology and Theology*, ed. Mark R. McMinn and Timothy R. Phillips (Downers Grove: InterVarsity Press, 2001), 254–75.

[48] Adapted from Brueggemann, *Theology of the Old Testament*, 685–8.

[49] Capps, *Reframing*, chapter 6, "The Inadequate Method of Job's Counselors."

assist him in returning to normal. Capps's study exposes the limitations and pitfalls of legalistic and traditionalist stances. The limitation of conventional wisdom is exposed as well in what Capps describes as status quo approaches for first-order change (change in the system). He goes on to consider God's response to Job as an instance of reframing, i.e., a transforming approach that can elicit second-order change (the change of the system as such). According to this view, God forces Job to look at his grief from a perspective that lies outside the vicious circle of his grief. In that light, faithful and effective pastoral counselors must be wise fools who know the art of reframing.[50] Capps thus reminds us of the multifaceted and dialectical character of biblical wisdom, and the precarious and paradoxical nature of our knowledge of God vis-à-vis the complexities of human life, especially in the face of limit. In the last analysis, it takes wisdom from above for us to be able to employ wisdom wisely in the ministry of pastoral counseling. The good news is that such wisdom is graciously available.

---

[50] Ibid., chapter 7, "God Reframes for Second-Order Change," and chapter 8, "The Wise Fool Reframes."

3 | *Reframing pastoral counseling*

ARMEN, A THIRTY-YEAR-OLD MEXICAN WOMAN, WAS referred to me for pastoral counseling because she was experiencing nervousness and depression. She was married to Oscar, thirty-two years old, and they had two children, eight and four years old. After having spent two years in prison for several episodes of physical violence and excessive drinking, Oscar was to be released in about a month.

During the two years of Oscar's incarceration, Carmen had made significant adjustments at home, having become, for the time being, a single parent and sole breadwinner for her family. In the process of learning new tasks and developing new skills, Carmen discovered that she was capable of far more than she had realized. Indeed, in a short period immediately after Oscar went to prison, she had found a job at a local manufacturing plant, learned to drive her husband's car, and started to learn English. Because she was an efficient and reliable employee, Carmen received two pay raises and a job promotion during the first year. In the second year, she was able to buy a car and began to consider buying a house instead of continuing to pay rent. The capacity to make important decisions after consulting relatives and friends had been an empowering source of satisfaction and self-esteem. Carmen was enjoying a new sense of personal worth, freedom, and accomplishment, despite difficulties along the way.

By the time we started counseling, Carmen was increasingly ambivalent about the prospect of returning to normal family life after the release of her husband. She and Oscar had remained in contact with periodic phone calls, regularly exchanged letters, and a few visits to the prison. The visits had included her older child, a boy who remembered his dad well and looked forward to having him at home again. Carmen still loved Oscar as her husband. She believed that his return could be the beginning of a new phase in their life together. He claimed to have become a much better person and had made promises about improved behavior and lifestyle after prison. On the other hand, she was not sure that Oscar could be trusted to accept the reality of her growth. She was anxious, because Oscar's return would certainly require adaptations of her, and very likely, disempowering compromises. Carmen felt guilty for sometimes imagining that she would be better off as a single parent. The resulting stress seemed to connect directly with her feeling nervous, as she described it (in Spanish, *nerviosa*, tense), and frequently depressed. Carmen and I had four counseling sessions before Oscar´s release.

Oscar was ready to meet me one-on-one soon after returning home. Understandably, he felt disoriented and frustrated: he could not drive until his license was legally reactivated, he had no job, and he needed to catch up with developments at home and elsewhere. He felt too dependent on Carmen, and at times overwhelmed by the changes that had taken place in the life of his family. He struggled with a sense of impotence mingled with shame, and he felt that Carmen was less emotionally close to him than he had expected. On the positive side were his good feelings associated with leaving prison life behind and reuniting with his wife and children.

Oscar was well aware of his need to learn new ways of appreciating and communicating with his wife. However, he was not sure that Carmen would be sufficiently patient and understanding, as he put it. Returning home had dramatically confirmed what he had begun to suspect while in prison, namely, that he could no longer take the marriage for granted and that he risked devastating loss. He realized clearly that much would depend on his choices under these difficult circumstances. It was less clear to Oscar that he needed to gain a wholesome sense of self, self-worth, and vocation as a man, and to rebuild hope on a deeper level. These and related issues became part of our agenda during three intense counseling sessions, which we followed with four sessions with them as a couple.

Meeting with Carmen and Oscar for marriage pastoral counseling was a special challenge, because at the time they were in very different places in their personal life journeys. The choices they had made during the last few years had led them in opposite directions, and their relationship was in serious trouble. Both were willing to make an effort to strengthen the marriage, although they expressed this good disposition differently (Oscar was more anxious for quick resolution, and Carmen was more deliberate and cautious). For my part, I needed to remain aware of the particularities of their Latino subculture with its values, practices, and expectations concerning men, women, marriage and the family, work, and faith.

As one might expect, we needed to focus first on how Oscar and Carmen might better communicate, understand, and mutually appreciate each other's experience, including anxieties, longings, fears, and expectations. They were then able to start reimaging their marriage and their family in more wholesome, hopeful, and fulfilling ways. Finally, they could agree on renegotiating their relationship with a new marriage covenant. This fundamental agreement included a stipulation that Oscar would participate in a community-based support group for Hispanic men focusing on conflict transformation. The couple further agreed to participate in marriage care and enrichment sponsored by their church. We agreed that the pastoral counseling experience had been fruitful, yet we recognized that it was only one part of the larger process leading to a better life.

In this chapter I argue in favor of reclaiming the essential role of pastoral counseling in the life of faith communities as well as outside the contours of the church narrowly defined. To this end I highlight the unique function of pastoral ministers as caregiving sages. I suggest that pastoral caregivers and other ministering people counsel those facing life's challenges (such as the need to make a key vocational decision) and struggles (such as the tragic death of a loved one) in the larger framework of congregational care. Indeed, they are called to such counseling, not as mental health professionals in the psychiatric sense, but as ministers of the gospel and worthy representatives of the caring, healing Christ.

Earlier I suggested that pastoral counseling focuses primarily on awakening, nurturing, and developing moral and spiritual intelligence. What specifically does this awakening look like when the biblical and theological base of pastoral counseling is reenvisioned in terms of wisdom in the light of God? How do pastoral counselors who operate in this framework understand themselves and their work? In the following pages, I present normative guidelines that provide a detailed answer to these questions. The guidelines are grouped into clusters that focus on six elements of my overall framework. Pastoral counseling that operates in the framework of wisdom in the light of God is therefore (a) viewed, practiced, and taught pastorally; (b) contextualized ecclesiologically; (c) centered on Jesus Christ as the wisdom of God; (d) grounded in Scripture; (e) viewed, practiced, and taught as a unique form of the re-creative process guided by the Spirit; and (f) oriented toward the reign of God. I use the pastoral counseling case[1] with which I opened the chapter to provide a backdrop for understanding each of these concepts in turn. In each of the sections, I connect the topic and a cluster of guidelines to my own pastoral counseling experience, as illustrated through the case study.

VIEWED AND PRACTICED PASTORALLY

At Maple City Health Care Center where I have volunteered on a regular basis for several years, staff made sure that Carmen and Oscar understood that I would relate to them as a pastoral counselor.[2] From the beginning of my volunteer service in the center, I established clarity about my role as pastoral counselor with the board and staff, and I have tried to serve consistently in

---

[1] Actually a composite of several similar situations from my experience in counseling low-income Hispanic people.

[2] The vision statement of this Goshen, Indiana, not-for-profit community health center states that its reason for being is to foster community in its neighborhood by promoting and providing accessible, affordable, integrated, quality primary health care. The center is run by a board made up of members of the community, including patients and others interested in promoting its vision. It offers discounts of up to ninety percent (based on income) for patients who qualify. The majority of the patients are lower-income, including many Latinos, especially people of Mexican descent. I fully share the vision that guides the center and I support its philosophy and approach to health care. I offer short-term pastoral counseling in English or Spanish, depending on the first language of the counselee. Roughly seventy percent of my counselees are women (because the preponderance of patients at the center are women and children, and also because women more readily seek counseling assistance, either for themselves or for other family members).

light of that understanding.[3] Carmen and Oscar collaborated with me, drawing on my pastoral care approach in ways that contributed to a resolution of the struggles they were facing individually and as a couple. My own contribution to that resolution was part of a larger effort which included other community and church-based services both during and after the time they participated in the pastoral counseling process. Indeed, whenever domestic violence is suspected or detected, counselors should make sure that the batterer is made fully accountable and that the victim receives adequate support. Under these circumstances, counseling the individual or the couple is not sufficient.[4]

Along with the knowledge, experience, and other resources I brought to pastoral counseling, I brought my own limitations, especially when counseling a woman[5] and people who are

---

[3] On formalizing my volunteer relationship with the center, I notified the denominational office responsible for ministerial credentialing in my denomination (Mennonite Church). I did so because I am an ordained minister, but also because I understand my work in pastoral counseling, whether in the context of my congregation or elsewhere, as a special form of pastoral care. As I discuss in the remainder of the chapter, I hold the view that pastoral counseling must be considered a ministry of the church in representing the caring, healing Christ. I also notified the pastors in my congregation and the small group to which my wife and I belong, which meets weekly for worship, prayer, study, and discernment. Thus, I have confirmed a primary relationship of accountability with the church—both broadly and narrowly speaking. I am also, of course, accountable to the people I serve and the community health center where I volunteer.

[4] According to Carmen's account, and according to the charges leading to Oscar's incarceration, domestic violence was a factor in this case, although it was not the main one. Nevertheless, I needed to keep in mind a number of guidelines of critical caregiving for the situation. For a good discussion of those guidelines, see Toinette M. Eugene and James Newton Poling, *Balm for Gilead: Pastoral Care for African American Families Experiencing Abuse* (Nashville: Abingdon Pr., 1998), chapter 6, "Pastoral Interventions with Victims and Survivors of Abuse," and chapter 7, "Pastoral Interventions with Perpetrators of Abuse."

[5] A number of valuable contributions have become available in recent years. See especially Christie Cozad Neuger, *Counseling Women: A Narrative, Pastoral Approach* (Minneapolis: Fortress Press, 2001). See also Jeanne Stevenson Moessner, ed., *Through the Eyes of Women: Insights for Pastoral Care* (Minneapolis: Fortress Press, 1996); Riet Bons-Storm, *The Incredible Woman: Listening to Women's Silences in Pastoral Care and Counseling* (Nashville: Abingdon Press, 1996); and

socioeconomically poor.[6] Thus, consultation and collaboration were essential dimensions of the multifaceted task of pastoral counseling. Collaboration with Carmen and Oscar became a way of applying practical theology for the sake of wisdom in the light of God. The task of counseling included a multiway conversation and hermeneutical process that engaged several perspectives and concerns. Together with issues pertaining to intrapersonal and interpersonal dynamics and family systems, I, along with Carmen and Oscar, approached spiritual and moral matters around such topics as grace, acceptance, repentance and forgiveness, gratitude, hope, commitment, and restorative justice.

Within the framework of wisdom in the light of God, pastoral counseling is defined and carried out as part of the church's ministry of care rather than as an arm of the psychotherapy industry and mental health professions. Further, it is primarily the disciplines of practical and pastoral theology that inform and reflect on pastoral counseling, both critically and constructively. I present three implications of these assertions in the guidelines that follow.

Pastoral counselors perceive themselves as caregiving sages. With such a vocational identity, pastoral ministers intentionally and uniquely partake in the orientation and purpose common to all ministry, namely, *sponsoring human emergence in the light of Christ.* Pastors must be vitally aware of this purpose while ministering to individuals, couples, families, and other small groups who bring to counseling their specific agendas of care. Whenever they authentically focus on this purpose, pastoral counselors may actually collaborate with God's Spirit in the formation and transformation of the emerging human self as spirit with a threefold pattern of vision, virtue, and vocation. That is to say, the rich and complex counseling agenda with its specific objectives in

---

Bonnie J. Miller-McLemore and Brita L. Gill-Austern, eds., *Feminist and Womanist Pastoral Theology* (Nashville: Abingdon Press, 1999).

[6] The following books are helpful: Ruby K. Payne, *A Framework for Understanding Poverty*, rev. ed. (Baytown, Tex.: RFT Publishing Company, 1998); and Patricia Minuchin, Jorge Colapinto, and Salvador Minuchin, *Working with Families of the Poor* (New York: Guilford Press, 1998). See especially James Newton Poling, *Render unto God: Economic Vulnerability, Family Violence, and Pastoral Theology* (Saint Louis: Chalice Press, 2002).

the face of counselees' special needs for care (from making difficult decisions to coping with trauma and loss), will always seek to also foster growth in the following dimensions: (a) the way of seeing and knowing, or the *vision* of the living God; (b) the way of being (character, heart), or the *virtue* of Christ; and (c) the way of living (play, work, service, and so on), or the *vocation* of the Spirit.[7]

Pastoral counselors are proficiently bilingual, able to speak the languages of psychology and of faith.[8] On the one hand, they must know the language of psychology and of counseling[9] in the dominant cultural framework, where psychology, especially in its psychotherapeutic expression, functions as conventional and pragmatic wisdom. Hence, pastoral counselors acquaint themselves with and use psychological views and resources related to human development, personality, and psychopathology, together with contributions from other human sciences (e.g., gender studies, sociocultural analysis). On the other hand, pastoral

---

[7] See the brief discussion of the overall purpose of pastoral counseling in chapter 1 of this book.

[8] For a systematic and clear treatment of the question of becoming bilingual concerning the perspectives, language, and understandings of psychology and theology, see Deborah van Deusen Hunsinger, *Theology and Pastoral Counseling: A New Interdisciplinary Approach* (Grand Rapids: Eerdmans, 1995). Hunsinger builds her case for interdisciplinary integrity and practical clarity on a Barthian approach to method.

[9] Carl R. Rogers, possibly the single most influential psychologist in the early stages of the modern pastoral counseling movement, wrote the classic work on the difference and continuity between counseling and psychotherapy (*Counseling and Psychotherapy* [Boston: Houghton Mifflin, 1942]). Normally, helping professionals view counseling as a relatively short process—one to five sessions—which tends to be problem-oriented; that is, it usually does not focus on personality structure and dynamics. A broad definition of psychotherapy includes the purpose of "amelioration of distress . . . relative to any or all of the following areas of disability or malfunction: cognitive functions (disorders of thinking), affective functions (suffering or emotional discomforts), or behavioral functions (inadequacy of behavior), with the therapist having some theory of personality's origins, development, maintenance and change along with some method of treatment logically related to the theory and professional and legal approval to act as a therapist" (Raymond J. Corsini and Danny Wedding, eds., *Current Psychotherapies*, 5th. ed. [Itasca, Ill.: F. E. Peacock, Publishers, Inc. 1995], 1).

counselors must be proficient in the language of faith and of theology. Therefore, they must be able to engage in pastoral diagnosis of spiritual issues, and to help people articulate and make sense of spiritual self-assessment and discernment.

Paul Pruyser is well known for his classic treatment of pastoral diagnosis and spiritual discernment. Pruyser underscores that those who are pastoral counselors must use their special training, knowledge, and experience to provide care from their unique pastoral and theological perspective. This approach is often neglected but nevertheless expected by those who turn to pastoral counselors. Pruyser also proposes specific guidelines focused on awareness of the holy, providence, faith, grace and gratefulness, repentance, community, and sense of vocation.[10] More recently, Nancy Ramsay has helpfully supplemented Pruyser's contribution.[11]

This bilingual understanding is particularly pertinent in our time, given the prominence of psychology and psychotherapy in the dominant culture. Addressing the question of the status and role of psychotherapy in our society, Robert Woolfolk starts with the notion that the therapeutic perspective is so endemic to contemporary life that its categories and assumptions shape our conceptions of what it is to be human. Woolfolk states, "Psychological theories now are taken for granted and have become our common sense and conventional wisdom."[12] He argues that psychotherapy will always involve wisdom as well as expertise, pedagogy as well as technology. Woolfolk uses wisdom here to mean practical know-how, primarily in the realm of relationships and emotions, including the capacity to discern goals and means and to engage in adequate decision making amid the complexities of everyday life. He thus juxtaposes the (Aristotelian) notion of *phronesis*—usually translated as practical

---

[10] Paul W. Pruyser, *The Minister As Diagnostician* (Philadelphia: Westminster Press, 1976). See also George Fitchett, *Assessing Spiritual Needs: A Guide for Caregivers* (Minneapolis: Augsburg Publishing House, 1993).

[11] Nancy J. Ramsay, *Pastoral Diagnosis: A Resource for Ministers of Care and Counseling* (Minneapolis: Fortress Press, 1998).

[12] Robert L. Woolfolk, *The Cure of Souls: Science, Values, and Psychotherapy* (San Francisco: Jossey-Bass, 1998), 1.

wisdom—with contemporary notions of practical and emotional intelligence.[13]

Vocationally and ideologically, pastoral counselors understand themselves primarily in terms of the ecclesial context and the life and work of the church. This is true even when pastoral counselors are not employed by a particular congregation, conference, or church-based institution. Further, pastoral counselors explicitly represent the historical and social reality of the church and the church's call to become a sacrament of the reign and the wisdom of God, a role I elaborate in the sections that follow. Pastoral counselors, therefore, are primarily, although by no means exclusively, accountable to the church, an observation that leads to my second group of normative guidelines.

CONTEXTUALIZED ECCLESIOLOGICALLY

Carmen and Oscar are Roman Catholic, but their participation in worship and other church activities had been sporadic. After Oscar went to prison, Carmen and the children began to attend church more regularly. Carmen experienced significant emotional, relational, and spiritual support in the church, especially because other relatives and friends also attended church services, although less regularly.[14] I affirmed such church involvement, and especially after Oscar's release from prison, I encouraged them both to regularly practice confession and communion (which many Hispanic men skip, even if they sometimes go to mass). Furthermore, I recommended to Oscar that he participate in a church-sponsored men's group that would address social interests and concerns related to work and health from a Christian perspective.

Strengthening a relationship with their faith community was a special counseling focus because their church participation had the potential to connect them with other sources of help. These resources in the church, as I understood them, included: first,

---

[13] Ibid., chapter 6, "Psychotherapy and Practical Knowledge."

[14] In counseling lower income people, I consistently find that, compared to those who are white and poor, Latinos seem to have more resources at their disposal in terms of both family networks and church participation (which for Latinos is mainly Roman Catholic).

worship, as the acknowledgement and celebration of the reign of God (including the affirmation of their belonging to God's people); second, community, as the embodiment of the spiritual family in the parish (including practices of mutual care and support); and third, mission, as participation in God's business in society (including practices of generosity and service). While participating in the church, they would not only receive the benefits of the church's life and ministry; they would also enjoy contributing their own gifts for the common good.

Reframing pastoral counseling as a ministry of the church implies that we take seriously the church's call to become a living sacrament[15] of the reign and the wisdom of God in the midst of history and culture. Here I use the term *sacrament* intentionally with the threefold meaning of sign, symbol, and means of grace. The church is called to become a truthful sign that points in the right direction, the direction of wholeness and the wise life. It is also called to become a symbol that faithfully re-presents—embodies in itself—the wisdom of God. It is called to become a fruitful means of grace, an instrument and agent of God's alternative wisdom in the world and for the sake of the world. Given its commitment to the way of Jesus and to ongoing discernment for the sake of faithfulness, the church is meant to become the wisdom community par excellence. That affirmation means, among other things, that we must view the faith community as the primary focus for care and the primary context and agent of care and counsel for the people of God. When pastoral counselors operate in the framework I am suggesting, at least three implications follow.

Pastoral counselors seek to minister primarily with a communal and contextual paradigm of pastoral care.[16] Within this framework clinical and other models can be selectively and critically

---

[15] In Latin America and elsewhere, reference to the church's call to become a sacrament of the life of God in the world and for the sake of the world became more frequent after the documents stemming from Vatican II were published.

[16] For a discussion of the communal-contextual paradigm, see John Patton, *Pastoral Care in Context* (Louisville: Westminster John Knox Press, 1993), part 1. For Patton, this interpretive model supplements and corrects the traditional and clinical paradigms in pastoral care.

appropriated. In this paradigm, pastoral care is viewed as the ministry of a faith community in light of its social context. The focus is on the caring community and the various contexts of care (instead of focusing exclusively or even primarily on pastoral care as the work of the ordained pastor). In other words, the guiding, nurturing, sustaining, reconciling, liberating, and healing dimensions of care are seen as a function of the whole church, not only for the sake of the well-being of its members but especially for the sake of the larger human community.[17]

Pastoral counselors and pastoral theologians acknowledge that God's call for the church is to manifest the revelatory presence and praxis of God's reign and God's wisdom. At the same time, they help the church discern the shape of this call and are themselves shaped by it. They identify and describe that call as the vocation of the church to become a good form[18] of human reality and wholeness in the light of God's reign and wisdom. I use the expression *good form* deliberately to include both an ethical (as in *righteous, morally good*) and aesthetic (as in *harmonious, beautiful in shape*) meaning. Of course, such good form always consists of a unique historical and contextualized embodiment of divine reign and wisdom. It is also clear, however, that no single faith community is capable of perfect form, of fully reflecting the wholeness of God's life and wisdom. The point is that faith communities are better and more beautiful to the extent that they take on the form of Christ. Pastoral counselors thus must acknowledge the ethical and aesthetic aspects of the church's identity and character as people of God, body of Christ, and temple of the Spirit.[19] To the extent

---

[17] For a discussion of distinctive Anabaptist commitments on the question of faith community care, including understandings of wellness and illness, care and cure, suffering and death, see Graydon F. Snyder, *Health and Medicine in the Anabaptist Tradition: Care in Community* (Valley Forge: Trinity Press International, 1995). For a helpful essay on the importance of focusing on the congregation, see Don S. Browning, "Pastoral Care and the Study of the Congregation," in *Beyond Clericalism: Congregation As a Focus for Theological Education,* ed. Joseph C. Hough Jr. and Barbara Wheeler (Atlanta: Scholars Press, 1988), 103–18.

[18] The term *good form,* used here metaphorically, is in a way analogous to the proposals of classic Gestalt psychology.

[19] The many helpful ecclesiological discussions of a theology of the Trinity include those in Leonardo Boff, *Holy Trinity, Perfect Community*, trans. Philip

that congregations become truthful, faithful, and fruitful sacramental communities, they also become revelation. Faith communities thus can provide grace-filled glimpses of the reign and the wisdom of God.

The formation and transformation of the faith community, in conformity with the wisdom and the praxis of God in the world, becomes a major concern for pastoral counselors. Thus the primary, although not exclusive, focus of pastoral counseling is to serve the formation and transformation process, a process involving every aspect of congregational life. This focus raises three fundamental questions about how pastoral counseling will interact with important aspects in the life of the church.

First, how does the practice of pastoral counseling enhance the worship life of the people of God? Pastoral counseling may enhance worship as people are helped to become more aware of and open to God's presence and grace; to appropriate the biblical story and biblical faith; to gain an understanding of the significance of worship; to appreciate the role of story, symbol, and ritual; and to learn the practices and disciplines of prayer, confession and repentance; etc.

Second, how does the practice of pastoral counseling help equip the church for building up God's family as the body of Christ? Pastoral counseling may contribute to this equipping when people are helped to become aware of themselves in God's presence, to embrace the biblical story of God's people and the historical tradition of the church, to gain interpersonal skills such as listening and communicating effectively, to learn to mediate conflicts and to resolve disputes, to develop attitudes and aptitudes for improving family life (or singleness), to learn to give and receive support and aid, to genuinely embrace marginalized groups and individuals (those who are unschooled, disabled, mentally ill, victims of abuse, and many others); etc.

Third, how does pastoral counseling empower the church as dwelling place of the Spirit to participate in God's mission in the

---

Berryman (Maryknoll: Orbis Books, 2000); Catherine Mowry LaCugna, *God for Us: The Trinity and the Christian Faith* (San Francisco: Harper and Row, 1991); and Miroslav Volf, *After Our Likeness: The Church in the Image of the Trinity* (Grand Rapids: Eerdmans, 1998). See also Mary Timothy Prokes, *Mutuality: The Human Image of Trinitarian Love* (New York: Paulist Press, 1993).

world and for the sake of the world? Pastoral counseling may contribute to this empowering as people are helped to recognize the Spirit's voice and work in the world; to receive and share God's loving invitation to the good news and good reality in Jesus Christ; to develop awareness, sensitivity, compassion, and solidarity in the face of prejudice based on gender, sexuality, race, culture, etc.; to join the struggle against injustice and oppression; to share and give generously; to serve (especially people who are poor, weak, disabled, and marginalized); to relate responsibly to the nonhuman environment; etc. As pastoral counselors engage in these ministries of enhancing, equipping, and empowering, our biblical and theological foundations point us always in the direction of Jesus Christ.

CENTERED ON JESUS CHRIST,
THE WISDOM OF GOD

As always in pastoral counseling settings, I sought to minister in the manner and in the name of Christ to Carmen and Oscar. This intention meant that the counseling process would be, from my perspective, a means of spiritual guidance. The overall purpose of my pastoral ministry to them would be to foster their spiritual formation and transformation in the light of Christ and of God's reign.

In counseling Carmen I was reminded of the special function of the Virgin of Guadalupe for many Mexican believers. Among the poor and marginalized, especially when the father is absent from the family, the experience of God tends to be mediated through an understanding of the Virgin Mary as Mother of God and archetype of sublime femininity (or mother archetype, in the Jungian sense). This is especially true when the prevailing images of Jesus Christ communicate either weakness and defeat or exalted and glorified afterlife triumph beyond history. In popular religiosity, Mary evokes the experience of refuge, protection, and consolation, without necessarily empowering poor women.[20] Something similar happens in the case of Jesus and men.

---

[20] Patricia C. Ulloa, "A Pastoral Psychology to Marginalized People: Experience of God in the Myth of the Virgin of Guadalupe," *American Journal of Pastoral Counseling* 2, no. 4 (1999): 45–64.

Therefore, one focus of pastoral counseling with Oscar and Carmen became the reconstruction of their understandings of Mary and Jesus in ways more faithful to the witness of the Gospels and as one dimension of the liberated and liberating Christian spirituality that Oscar and Carmen needed.

Reframing pastoral counseling as wisdom in the light of God implies an affirmation that Christ is the center of this practice of care. It also implies that Christ is the center of the critical and constructive (pastoral) theological reflection that must stem from the practice of pastoral care, and undergird and evaluate it as well. A number of implications follow when we understand pastoral counseling in this light.

Pastoral counselors seek to be guided by a Christ-inspired vision of human becoming, humanization—human wholeness and fullness of life, and wholesome and wise living. Hence, they must find explicit connections between their actual ministry practice and the confession that Jesus Christ embodies the life and wisdom of God and makes known to us God's will for human conduct and destiny. It is crucial to be clear and consistent about this confession. The Christ-inspired vision for human becoming must be considered together with holistic views of salvation and shalom. Pastoral counselors thus appropriate and integrate these fundamental theological convictions about the work of Christ for the re-creation of our full humanity.

Pastoral counselors are concerned with manifold expressions of faithfulness and growth in the life of faith (discipleship). They seek to relate this longed-for faithfulness and growth to rich and complex counseling settings and agendas. Many situations make pastoral counseling desirable or necessary in the face of existential challenges and struggles (for instance, the need to discern the best alternatives while making significant choices, dealing with interpersonal conflicts, needing to cope with pain and death, or confronting abuse). Within these occasions for ministry, the reflection of pastoral theologians and the work of ministers as caregiving sages must also establish meaningful connections between presenting issues and growth in the life of Christian faith. Interestingly, we can see a correlation between the formation and transformation of the church in worship, community, and mission, on the one hand, and the formation and transformation of the human spirit in its vision, virtue, and vocation, on the other hand. Communally as well as personally, taking on the form of Christ is what matters. Spiritual growth is thus understood in light of our conviction that Christ is "the power of God and the wisdom of God . . . who became for us wisdom from God, and righteousness and sanctification and redemption" (1 Cor. 1:24b, 30b). This is wisdom in which believers share, for "we have the mind of Christ" (1 Cor. 2:16b).

As representatives of Christ, pastoral counselors long for their own growth into Christ and seek to relate and to practice with Christian character. Pastoral counseling in a Christian manner assumes several interrelated dimensions of identity and character on the part of the caregiver. These include a Christian frame of mind or way of knowing, a Christian heart or way of loving and being, and a Christian sense of vocation or way of living and working. Pastoral counselors seek explicitly to establish pastoral care relationships in the name and in the Spirit of Christ. Obviously, one might expect that something similar will occur with Christians who work in the practical human sciences such as education or applied psychology. There, too, one would hope that professing Christian practitioners practice in a Christian manner and reflect Christian character.[21] However, those who are pastoral Christian counselors will represent the church explicitly. Further, in their pastoral relationships they will deliberately represent the caring Christ who guides and nurtures, sustains, reconciles, liberates, and heals those in need of God's saving grace in the midst of their existential challenges

---

[21] Expressed in different terms, this is the commitment of members of the American Association of Christian Counselors and the Christian Association of Psychological Studies; it is also a stated principle of doctoral programs in clinical psychology such as those of Fuller Theological Seminary and Wheaton College. Mark R. McMinn says it nicely in his book, *Psychology, Theology and Spirituality in Christian Counseling* (Wheaton: Tyndale House Publishers, 1997): "The Christian counselors best prepared to help people are those who are not only highly trained in counseling theory and techniques and in theology but also personally trained to reflect Christian character inside and outside of the counseling office. This character cannot be credentialed with graduate degrees or learned in the classroom; it comes from years of faithful training in the spiritual disciplines— prayer, studying Scripture, solitude, fasting, corporate worship" (14).

and struggles.[22] Last but not least, I argue that the practice and the theory of pastoral counseling have much to offer Christian counselors and psychotherapists, although almost always the reverse has been assumed—that pastoral counselors will take their cues from secular counselors and psychotherapists. It must, I assert, be a two-way street.

GROUNDED IN SCRIPTURE

In counseling Carmen and Oscar, I was required to listen pastorally to their stories and hopes in the light of the gospel and the reign and wisdom of God. Glimpses of divine reign and wisdom were already apparent in their lives and in their faith community. Sometimes in unexpected places (such as home and family, the workplace, and even the prison) love, peace, freedom, and justice were present, even if in small measures. I needed to recognize and name those glimpses, together with the windows on God's reign and wisdom that Scripture presents. I needed to critically appropriate and truthfully mediate the Christian tradition that shapes my pastoral care ministry. Further, I needed to help Carmen and Oscar make connections between their personal stories and hopes, and the larger Christian story and hope, in ways that would illuminate their lives and point to a better future for the two of them. In other words, I had to lead the kind of hermeneutical conversation that locates pastoral counseling in the larger field of practical theology.

Carmen and Oscar were not very familiar with the Bible. Discussion of biblical material was not part of our counseling agenda, except for brief references to the portraits of Mary and Jesus in the Gospels. Nevertheless, throughout our individual and joint sessions I remained aware that we were engaged in a discernment process that defines biblical wisdom as theologically interpreted human experience and as a way of doing theology. Indeed, I sought to guide Carmen and Oscar according to the way of wisdom in the light of God.

---

[22] For a classic affirmation of this position, see Wayne J. Oates, *The Christian Pastor* (Philadelphia: Westminster Press, 1951); see also Oates's *Protestant Pastoral Counseling* (Philadelphia: Westminster Press, 1962), in which he formulates his view of pastoral counseling from within a free church tradition.

When pastoral counseling is centered on wisdom in the light of God, its biblical foundation and inspiration are reflected and expressed in the importance given to Scripture. In the following paragraphs, I highlight four interrelated ways that the Bible's centrality manifests itself. These four guidelines help ground pastoral counseling firmly in Scripture, an attribute that is essential to the wisdom framework.

Pastoral counselors work with a biblically informed wisdom framework and perspective. This framework will be in tune with the pastoral counselor's confessional affirmation concerning Scripture. My theological and denominational tradition considers Scripture "the fully reliable and trustworthy standard for Christian faith and life" (which, I would add, we understand and interpret in harmony with Jesus Christ, the Wisdom of God and Word become flesh), "as we are led by the Holy Spirit in the church."[23] A biblically informed framework and perspective will decisively fashion the pastoral counselor's view of reality, knowing, and truth; human nature and destiny; formation and transformation; the nature of the good; human wholeness and wellness; and daily wise living, loving, and working.

Pastoral counselors, like teachers and preachers, give due consideration to the teachings, narratives, poetry, prophecy, and other biblical materials, as these expressions of the written Word illuminate and address their counselees' existential challenges and struggles. The particular setting and ministry art of pastoral counseling will condition how biblical material is considered. A variety of approaches is possible.[24] However, the Bible is not merely a

---

[23] "Scripture," Article 4 of *Confession of Faith in a Mennonite Perspective* (Scottdale and Waterloo: Herald Press, 1995), 21. It makes a difference what we believe about the Bible and biblical interpretation. I trust that readers will think through personal convictions about Scripture in light of their own theological and denominational traditions.

[24] See, for instance, Donald Capps, *Biblical Approaches to Pastoral Counseling* (Philadelphia: Westminster Press, 1981); *Reframing: A New Model of Pastoral Care* (Minneapolis: Fortress Press, 1990); "The Bible's Role in Pastoral Care and Counseling: Four Basic Principles," *Journal of Psychology and Christianity* 3, no. 4 (1985): 5–14; and "Bible, Pastoral Use and Interpretation of," in *Dictionary of Pastoral Care and Counseling,* ed. Rodney J. Hunter (Nashville: Abingdon Press,

helpful tool or resource for pastoral counseling; it contributes decisively to the very goals, process, and content of this ministry art. Thus pastoral counselors affirm the power of Scripture as an agent of disclosure and of change. Simultaneously, they need to remain aware of the specific situations encountered in counseling and be sensitive to the particular needs and growth potential of those seeking care. In any event, the Bible is not conformed to counseling or therapy goals but rather the reverse. Any psychological and psychotherapeutic theories and approaches used in pastoral counseling must be consistent with the power of the Bible to disclose wisdom in the light of God. This guideline reflects an understanding that the Bible is the one essential book of the church. It is also congruent with the normative convictions of our faith tradition concerning Scripture.[25]

Pastoral counselors give special attention to a unique hermeneutical counseling process with the goal of wise discernment, wise decision making, and wise living.[26] They acknowledge that the counseling process, when viewed as a dynamic encounter with the living documents and narratives of people's lives, includes an inductive structure that is analogous to reading the biblical text in terms of asking (observing), assessing (judging), and applying (acting). They also acknowledge that the counseling process consists of a

---

1990), 82–4. See also Edward P. Wimberly, *Using Scripture in Pastoral Counseling* (Nashville: Abingdon Press, 1994).

[25] "Scripture," Article 4 of *Confession of Faith in a Mennonite Perspective.* The guideline is also consistent with affirmations about the place and interpretation of the Bible found in the statement of philosophy of theological education at the seminary where I teach: "As teachers of the church and servants of the Word, we accept the Scripture as the primary measure of what we teach in all theological disciplines. . . . It means that we seek to have the categories of our disciplines, the history and ministries of the church, and our interpretation of the contemporary world measured and formed by Scripture" (*Ministerial Formation and Theological Education in Mennonite Perspective* [Elkhart, Ind.: Associated Mennonite Biblical Seminary, 1993], 6).

[26] Discussions of hermeneutics and pastoral care and counseling, and pastoral and practical theology, can be found in Donald Capps, *Pastoral Care and Hermeneutics* (Philadelphia: Fortress Press, 1984); Charles V. Gerkin, *Re-Visioning Pastoral Counseling in a Hermeneutical Mode* (Nashville: Abingdon Press, 1984); and *Prophetic Pastoral Practice: A Christian Vision of Life Together* (Nashville: Abingdon Press, 1991).

unique form of hermeneutical circulation engaging not only the counselee's personal agenda in family and sociocultural settings but also the agenda of the reign of God in dialogue with that of both church and society. Pastoral counseling within this guideline rejects the literalist, rationalist, and fundamentalist use of the Bible in counseling, as presented by some well-known authors.[27] On the contrary, pastoral counselors seek to guide a multi-way conversation which involves the story and the vision graciously revealed in Scripture and in Jesus Christ, and people's personal and family stories and visions in the midst of their social situations and life's challenges and struggles. In short, a process that is truly practical and theological must take place.

In the counseling setting, pastoral counselors play a role that is analogous to the role of teachers, preachers, and spiritual directors: they must act as grace-filled and worthy intermediaries in the interaction of the *counsel of God* with the counselees. I do not intend the counsel of God here to mean merely godly advice; authoritarian, legalistic-moralistic, and paternalistic instruction; or mere words of wisdom (although, indeed, instruction and words of wisdom are normally called for in pastoral counseling). Rather, by the *counsel of God* I mean the very reality of divine presence, grace, and power.[28] Given such a privilege and responsibility, therefore, *pastoral counselors seek to nurture their own spirituality and to grow in their own biblically grounded ways of seeing and knowing, loving and being, and living and working.* Their personal journey of discipleship, their own life-walk on the way of wisdom, must also be grounded in Scripture.

---

[27] See, for example, Jay E. Adams, *The Use of Scripture in Counseling* (Grand Rapids: Baker Books, 1975). See also *The Journal of Biblical Counseling,* a publication that promotes the principles of the biblical counseling movement. According to its editors, it is dedicated to helping believers apply the Bible wisely to problems in living, think about life with an accurate reality map, and meet others with faithful and effective help.

[28] On this point, see Ray S. Anderson, *Christians Who Counsel: The Vocation of Wholistic Therapy* (Grand Rapids: Zondervan Publishing House, 1990), especially chapter 6, "The Word of God As Empowerment for Change."

CARRIED OUT AS A RE-CREATIVE PROCESS
GUIDED BY THE SPIRIT

Pastoral counseling with Carmen and Oscar was a collaborative process carried out in three phases—with Carmen, with Oscar, and with them as a couple. I experienced the counseling relationship as an opportunity to join their life briefly at a critical juncture, having been welcomed by them as a neighbor and guide for their journey. For this we needed to establish together a context of rapport nurtured by mutual trust. The process unfolded very differently for each of them, beginning with the startling contrast between Carmen's sense of agency and Oscar's debilitating confusion about his status and future. Carmen's recently developed voice needed validation; Oscar, in contrast, needed to find a new voice.

Collaboration with Carmen and Oscar was indispensable to help them move from telling their stories to becoming the authors of a new story, both individually and as a couple. The movement consisted of tasks involving memory, critical interpretation, and imagination. The process of discernment included moments of intuition and discovery that encouraged Carmen and Oscar to make choices in light of their personal and joint agenda. Further, we needed to ascertain together whether the emerging sense of direction actually pointed to living more wisely, and if it did, we needed to consider how to sustain the intended changes in the days ahead, beyond the pastoral counseling relationship.

I knew all along that our collaboration was occurring in partnership with the Spirit of God, who is the Spirit of truth, wisdom, and healing. With that realization I prayed for myself and I prayed for Carmen and Oscar between our sessions and often, silently, during our sessions. It was only at the end of each of the three counseling phases that I felt it appropriate to suggest that I pray with them.

Wisdom in the light of God is a gift we can receive and mediate by divine grace. Reframed within the way of wisdom, pastoral counseling therefore challenges pastoral theologians and counselors to consider seeking, discerning, and appropriating authentic signs and expressions of wisdom. Interdisciplinary exploration leads us to look at the counseling process as a specialized version of the creative process, including its re-creating, healing, and liberating dimensions. Guided by the Holy Spirit this process must be theologically reinterpreted and practically appropriated in Christian ministry.[29] Two related guidelines follow.

Pastoral counselors seek to participate in God's three-dimensional praxis of (1) guiding, nurturing, and sustaining; (2) liberating, reconciling, and healing; and (3) renewing and empowering. By exercising careful spiritual discernment and theological reflection in the context of pastoral counseling, together with actual counseling work in specific ministry settings, pastoral counselors have the opportunity to participate in God's praxis. Consciously and prayerfully, they seek to be inspired, sustained, and directed by the Spirit of God. Further, they perceive their work as caregiving sages as one of partnership and collaboration with the Spirit.[30] In other words, they know that by themselves they cannot effect growth in wise living and human emergence in the light of Christ, for God alone gives healing and growth, as the apostle Paul reminded the Corinthians (1 Cor. 3:7b). Yet they also know that, precisely in their role as counselors, they have a unique opportunity to sponsor growth as they are present to people in ways conducive to collaboration with the Spirit, that is, with compassionate initiative, hospitable inclusiveness, gentle empowerment, and a generous invitation to partnership and community. They may thus counsel fully attuned to the divine counselor and advocate who reminds us of Jesus' way and guides us into all truth (John 14:26; 16:13).[31]

---

[29] Concerning this normative guideline I am indebted to James E. Loder, *The Transforming Moment*, 2d ed. (Colorado Springs: Helmers & Howard, 1989); and also *The Logic of the Spirit: Human Development in Theological Perspective* (San Francisco: Jossey-Bass, 1998). Loder's pioneering interdisciplinary work includes a proposed way to appreciate the God-initiated and sustained collaborative endeavor engaging the Holy Spirit and the human spirit in settings such as those of counseling and psychotherapy.

[30] On this point of ministry practice as collaboration with the Spirit, see June A. Yoder, "Collaborative Preaching: Persuasion and the Spirit in Close-Up" (D.Min. thesis, Bethany Theological Seminary, 1991).

[31] Discussions of the Holy Spirit for the field of pastoral care can be found in Marvin G. Gilbert and Raymond T. Brock, eds., *Theology and Theory*, vol. 1 of *The Holy Spirit and Counseling* (Peabody: Hendrickson Publishers, Inc., 1985); John

Closely connected with the previous guideline, *pastoral counseling must be viewed, practiced, and taught as fundamentally analogous to other practices of ministry such as teaching, preaching, mentoring, and spiritual guidance.* In light of this principle, we discern a structural continuity among the diverse ministry arts; these ministry arts have much in common because they all share an undergirding pattern which is essential to foster learning, conviction, formation, and transformation. The dynamics of collaboration with the Spirit include the following dimensions and movements that define the common pattern and design:[32] (a) encounter and contemplation, which make it possible to create safe spaces and contexts of rapport for discipling and caring ministries; (b) engagement and expression, which invite others to share their own stories and visions in their own voices; (c) reflection and discernment, including the kind of search or "scanning" that allows for the creative work of the imagination; (d) explicit access to the wisdom of the faith community; (e) appropriation, which invites people to understand, judge, and make decisions; and (f) commitment, which includes guidance for acting on choices and commitments, together with expectation of shared accountability, for the common purpose of wise living.

ORIENTED TOWARD THE REIGN OF GOD

Counseling Carmen and Oscar would entail much more than an occasion of care ministry focused on personal and interpersonal levels, as I have learned from my work with Hispanic and lower-income people. I first needed to appreciate the reality of their lives in the context of the dominant North American Midwestern culture, in which Latino immigrants are second-class people, a

---

Kie Vining, *Spirit-Centered Counseling* (East Rockaway, N.Y.: Cummings & Hathaway, 1995); and John Kie Vining, ed., *Pentecostal Caregivers . . . Anointed to Heal* (East Rockaway, N.Y.: Cummings & Hathaway, 1995).

[32] I am intentionally associating my proposal with Thomas Groome's and James Loder's work at this point. See Groome, *Sharing Faith,* especially the applications of his shared praxis approach to several ministry forms, in the last part of the book. I am also connecting it with Maria Harris's paradigm for teaching in *Teaching and Religious Imagination: An Essay in the Theology of Teaching* (San Francisco: Harper & Row, 1987), chapter 2, which includes these steps: contemplation, engagement, form-giving, emergence, and release.

status with sociocultural, economic, and political implications. Further, I needed to also understand their behavior in terms of their being embedded in a Hispanic culture. In turn, I needed this consideration of society and culture to dialogue critically with the framework that defines my ministry—the ethical, political, and eschatological vision of the reign and the wisdom of God.

I included in my approach an intentional effort to confront the conventional and pragmatic wisdom of both the dominant culture and the Latino subculture at the points where they promote and reinforce diverse forms of violence, oppression, and marginalization. These cultures clearly required confrontation, for example, regarding certain manifestations of patriarchy that were affecting Carmen and Oscar in different ways. Therefore, a key dimension of the counseling agenda was to help them resist and transform those damaging cultural structures within themselves, in their marital and family relationships, and beyond.

Both the promise and the limitations of pastoral counseling became more apparent as I worked with Carmen and Oscar. Consequently, our collaborative endeavors together would need intentional reinforcing, augmenting, and supplementing in other settings in the church and in the local community as they moved toward a better and more fulfilling life.

The symbol of God's reign points to the vision and promise of the commonwealth of freedom, justice, peace, welfare, and wholeness which is primarily a divine gift and which will ultimately be fully realized beyond history. *Pastoral counselors seek to appropriate and reflect the conviction that the ultimate context of wisdom, including wisdom in discernment, guidance and growth, reconciliation, healing, liberation and wholeness, is the culture of the reign of God.*[33] I asserted earlier that partaking of that culture calls for and at the same time fosters wise living in the light of God. Affirmation of the biblical and theological foundations and framework that I have presented, especially focusing on the

---

[33] For this way of articulating the principle I am indebted to Alvin C. Dueck, *Between Jerusalem and Athens: Ethical Perspectives on Culture, Religion, and Psychotherapy* (Grand Rapids: Baker Books, 1995), especially part 1. A similar case is made by Ray Anderson, in *Christians Who Counsel*, chapter 5, "The Kingdom of God As Therapeutic Context."

connection between God's reign and divine wisdom,[34] suggests two final guidelines for pastoral counseling as a ministry of the church within the culture of the reign of God.

Pastoral counselors, in light of their vision of God's commonwealth of freedom, justice, and peace, remain aware that their ministry work as caregivers always takes place in the social and cultural context of the church and the larger society. They claim that the reign of God is a social reality and a culture, a way of life that may take form in any historical culture. Further, they claim that God's reign can adapt and correct all other existing cultural forms (including, of course, the church's): relationships, systems, practices, power dynamics, values, beliefs, and ideals can be addressed, challenged, affirmed, or transformed in the light of the wisdom of God. By drawing on the threefold declaration of Jesus as the way, the truth, and the life (John 14:6), Ray Anderson highlights three components of the reign of God that serve as environment and horizon for the Christian counselor: (a) discernment that makes meaning and coherence available to those seeking care (i.e., the way that Jesus came to be and to share); (b) a righteousness embodied in the moral structures of the people of God (i.e., the truth Jesus came to be and to create); and (c) a sense of identity communicated through a story in which each person participates, with a hope that compels people of faith to value life and to love community (i.e., the life that Jesus came to be and to give).[35]

Pastoral counselors become ethical agents of the culture of the reign of God. As such, they practice as "cartographers and tour guides for a better culture."[36] Given their primary loyalty to the reign of God, they seek to give consistent and specific consideration to the ethical dimensions of their ministry. Those ethical dimensions include not only professional ethics, personal values, and norms

---

[34] Scholars such as John Dominic Crossan suggest that the kingdom of God language of Jesus also can be considered in the context of the wisdom tradition and theology. See *The Historical Jesus: The Life of a Mediterranean Jewish Peasant* (San Francisco: Harper San Francisco, 1991), 287–92.

[35] Anderson, *Christians Who Counsel*, especially 86–102.

[36] Dueck uses this phrase in his discussion of psychotherapists as ethicists, in *Between Jerusalem and Athens*, 13.

narrowly viewed, but also the communal and sociopolitical import of their ministry.[37]

Finally, the embodiment of God's reign can take place on different levels and in diverse forms, as Alvin Dueck suggests. As an ethical culture, the story and the vision of God's reign can provide the narrative and the visional context for the counselor as ethicist. The reign of God is our re-creating, liberating, and culture-creating story and vision; it provides the ethos and ethic for counseling and a critical and political perspective on our western culture. The church as community of wisdom is called to become a living sign of God's reign in its practice and its reflection on what it means to be human in the twenty-first century. Individuals and families are invited to partake of life in the light of God's reign. The character of the ministering person viewed as a caregiving sage is especially to be shaped by the rituals, the narratives, and the discernment of the Christian faith community.[38]

The metaphor of wisdom in the light of God has given a solid foundation for reaffirming the biblical and theological basis of pastoral counseling and its place as a ministry of the church. With this foundation in mind, I have outlined in this chapter specific guidelines for pastoral counselors who operate within the framework I have proposed. Pastoral counselors who appropriate these guidelines are reclaiming pastoral counseling as a form of practical theology and a specialized setting for the practice of wisdom. For this purpose, I propose and explicate a new definition of this special form of pastoral care. This definition of

---

[37] In the field of pastoral care and counseling, there have been promising developments in this regard in recent years, as documented, for example, in Pamela D. Couture and Rodney J. Hunter, eds., *Pastoral Care and Social Conflict* (Nashville: Abingdon Press, 1995); George M. Furnish, *The Social Context of Pastoral Care* (Louisville: Westminster John Knox Press, 1994); Jeanne Stevenson Moessner, ed., *Through the Eyes of Women: Insights for Pastoral Care* (Minneapolis: Fortress Press, 1996); and James Newton Poling, *Render unto God: Economic Vulnerability, Family Violence, and Pastoral Theology* (St. Louis: Chalice Press, 2002).

[38] Adapted from Dueck, *Between Jerusalem and Athens*, Part 1. I deliberately add *vision* to *story* because I want to emphasize more than Dueck does the future-oriented, hope-filled, prophetic, eschatological, and utopian dimensions involved in, and elicited by, the biblical symbol of the reign of God.

pastoral counseling is the subject of my final chapter, to which I now turn.

4 | *Reenvisioning pastoral counseling*

THE REFRAMED VIEW OF PASTORAL COUNSELING OUTLINED IN the preceding chapter offers a way of viewing, practicing, and teaching pastoral counseling that is significantly different—both more appropriate and more pertinent—than the views, practices, and teachings provided by the medical or psychiatric model. This reframed view calls for a new definition of pastoral counseling as a special form and setting of pastoral care in the ministry of the church.

Pastoral counseling is a special art and form of the church's ministry of care.[1] *In pastoral counseling, human emergence is uniquely sponsored through a distinctive way of walking with individuals, couples, family members, or small groups as they face life's challenges and struggles. The overall goal, simply stated, is that they may live wisely in the light of God.* In the last chapter I introduced part of this definition: pastoral counseling is a specialized form of pastoral care which partakes of the overall purpose of ministry, namely, to sponsor human emergence in the light of Jesus Christ and the reign of God. This chapter presents a discussion, in some detail, of the remainder: a distinctive way of walking with others as they face life's challenges and struggles, that they may live wisely in the light of God.

A DISTINCTIVE WAY OF WALKING WITH OTHERS

Karen and Raúl were in their mid-twenties when they began to consider marriage, after a couple years of learning to know and love each other. Each had rebounded well from a previous unfulfilling special friendship. The two became engaged and set a date for the wedding during the following summer, seven months away.

---

[1] Definitions of pastoral care and pastoral counseling can be found in the introduction.

Not long after their engagement, both Karen and Raúl began to feel uneasy about their decision and uncertain about their readiness for marriage. Friends told them they were having normal pre-wedding jitters or cold feet, and predicted that they would soon become excited about the wedding and their future life together. However, Karen and Raúl were not sure. After all, their family and sociocultural backgrounds were very different, and from time to time they had had serious misunderstandings and conflicting expectations of each other. Karen took the initiative to seek pastoral counseling, with Raul's support, because some days she felt deeply ambivalent about the prospect of getting married.

Karen's initial session with her pastor provided an occasion to express her anxieties freely, to identify certain fears and hopes with more clarity. It also allowed her to own her need to prepare more deliberately for marriage (should their plans remain unchanged), both internally and interpersonally with Raúl. The pastor, a woman in her early forties, suggested that it would be helpful to give Raúl an opportunity to meet with her, too, before deciding whether further pastoral counseling with the couple would be advisable.

At first Raúl appeared less convinced than Karen that they as a couple had work to do on growing edges in their relationship. The pastor suggested beginning with consideration of their family stories and how these stories had shaped their lives. Eventually, she thought, they might also focus on ways to strengthen their relational dispositions and skills during the period of their engagement. Raúl was committed to Karen and their relationship, and chose to be an active participant in the counseling process.

Karen and Raúl met with their pastor for counseling once a week for a month and a half. The pastor would provide further guidance in a series of pre-wedding sessions planned for early summer.

The phrase *a distinctive way of walking with others* suggests that counselors become fellow travelers and companions—wise guides and cartographers in the personal journeys of their counselees. Walking in this way consists of a certain kind of partnership in counseling settings, that is, settings that are relatively structured in the sense of agreed-on goals, scheduled conversations, and appropriate use of methods and resources. The walk and journey metaphors are particularly meaningful when considered in light of the ministry of Jesus. Drawing on Jesus' ministry as paradigm, I present a brief illustration from the Gospel records, followed by a discussion of the uniqueness of the pastoral counseling relationship.

A PROTOTYPICAL GOSPEL CASE

The post-resurrection narrative of the journey to Emmaus (Luke 24:13–35) is a wonderful illustration of what it means *to minister on the way, in the manner of Christ*. Such ministry involves both discipling and caring dimensions.[2] In the story, we encounter two disciples who are experiencing an overwhelming sense of loss while discussing the events leading to the bitter end at Golgotha. These two common folk are leaving Jerusalem with a sense of defeat; they are confused and plagued by doubt, fear, and anxiety. Their disillusionment is mingled with hope, however, because of news they have heard from some women of their group. As a result, they have many questions and are disoriented. The struggle for understanding motivates the two disciples to welcome the stranger, to receive his ministry to them on the road, and to offer him hospitality. In sum, their open disposition and collaboration with the stranger are crucial in the ensuing work of care and discipling, which in turn fosters their transformation.

Jesus, the wise caregiver, fittingly comes second in the story and does not call attention to himself. On the contrary, he becomes the disciples' neighbor by entering into their reality on their terms. He invites the disciples to tell their story, to own their pain, and to confess their crushed dreams and hopes for a better future. In due time Jesus also makes it possible for the disciples to place the social context and circumstances of their lives alongside the witness of Scripture and against the horizon of liberation in

---

[2] Two applications of the Emmaus story are especially helpful. Thomas H. Groome uses the account to illustrate his "shared praxis approach" in *Christian Religious Education: Sharing Our Story and Vision* (San Francisco: Harper & Row, 1981), 136–7, 207–23. James E. Loder analyzes the story in his "logic of transformation" model in *The Transforming Moment*, 2d ed. (Colorado Springs: Helmers & Howard, 1989), 97–114.

the light of God. He then confronts conventional wisdom about the Messiah with the wisdom and power of God in Christ and the paradox of the cross. Jesus thus plays a mediating role in the interface between human experience and divine will graciously revealed afresh. In a variety of ways, he engages the total self of each disciple while inviting them both to be partners in the process and respecting their freedom to make choices (for instance, when he allows them to become hosts and to share their bread, thus becoming literally his companions). Finally, Jesus disengages at the opportune time. The disciples are reoriented and empowered to fulfill their vocation in a community that is getting ready to participate in the work of the Spirit in the world. They are able to affirm that they have faced their struggle while walking with Jesus on the road to Emmaus, and as a result have become wiser in the light of God.

A SPECIAL KIND OF RELATIONSHIP

The relationship of the pastoral counselor as a fellow traveler includes dimensions of witness, sponsorship, accompaniment, critical caring, engagement, and incarnational presence. On the one hand, the counseling relationship is one of dialogical collaboration. On the other hand, this relationship is asymmetrical and not mutual, because counselors by definition guide the process. There is an acknowledged distinction between care-seeker and caregiver. In describing this asymmetry, James E. Dittes understands the pastoral counselor as a unique kind of witness. He views pastoral counseling as a stringent ministry of witnessing which calls for four ascetic renunciations on the part of counselors: renouncing the expectations of everyday etiquette; the expectations of intimate relationships; the expectations of performance, proficiency, prowess, and achievement; and the expectations of clerical identity as conventionally regarded.[3] The witness metaphor is helpful but insufficient, however, when our

---

[3] James E. Dittes, *Pastoral Counseling: The Basics* (Louisville: Westminster John Knox Press, 1999), chapter 3. Says Dittes, "Fundamentally, the pastoral counselor does not try to 'do' anything and is not struggling to make something happen, to make repairs, or to make changes. The intent of pastoral counseling is more profound than that. The pastoral counselor witnesses . . . to the fullness of [the counselee's] life" (57).

biblical and theological foundations identify pastoral counselors as caregiving sages. We need additional images, such as the figure of the sponsor in the early church. Sponsors guide spiritual formation by offering maps and models as they walk alongside pilgrims. They encourage, challenge, and enable pilgrims on the road of daily life so that they may live well—wisely—in the light of God.

Another image for the counseling relationship is that of accompaniment. By accompanying others, counselors guide a process that normally unfolds in phases of exploration, discernment, interpretation, support, and so on. Accompaniment must happen in the spirit and style of critical caring, a concept developed by Valerie DeMarinis. She proposes that we understand the term *critical* in terms of both careful judgment and crucial intervention; both definitions are needed to link thought and action. The term *caring* she understands as appropriate concern. DeMarinis thus summarizes, "Critical caring signifies, therefore, the ability for careful judgment and appropriate concern to work together for crucial intervention."[4] The uniqueness of pastoral counseling as a means of critical caring reminds us of what the clinical paradigm, with its understanding of psychodynamics, especially concerning the counseling relationship, has to contribute to pastoral care and counseling.

Pervasively influenced by psychoanalytic and Rogerian approaches to psychotherapy, the practice and theory of pastoral counseling has tended to center on the counseling relationship as the key to growth, transformation, and healing. That is still the view of many practitioners and authors,[5] and one can gain much from this view while benefiting from the perspective of counseling as a way of wisdom. It is indeed crucial for pastoral counselors as caregiving sages and guides to remain aware of the particular

---

[4] Valerie DeMarinis, *Critical Caring: A Feminist Model of Pastoral Psychology* (Louisville: Westminster John Knox Press, 1993), 17; see especially the introduction and first section.

[5] See, for example, John Patton, *Pastoral Counseling: A Ministry of the Church* (Nashville: Abingdon Press, 1983), chapter 7, "What Heals?—Relationship in Pastoral Counseling"; and Richard Dayringer, *The Heart of Pastoral Counseling: Healing through Relationship*, rev. ed. (New York: Haworth Pastoral Press, 2000).

dynamics involved in their relationships with counselees—
transference (and counter-transference) and resistance (and
counter-resistance), for instance. It is likewise crucial to use this
awareness constructively to guide the counseling process.
However, pastoral counselors must also be aware of three
potential pitfalls of overemphasizing the counseling relationship
as such. First, the main counseling foci are challenges or struggles
presented by counselees, rather than the counselee's relationship
with the pastoral counselor. Most pastoral counseling is short-
term, so a focus on the counseling relationship should not
dominate. Second, the relational view of pastoral counseling, a
view that assumes the primary nature of the counseling
relationship, may create the conditions for boundary violations
(including sexual misconduct) and may underestimate the
resources of counselees themselves.[6] Third, an overemphasis on
the counseling relationship, narrowly focused, as the key to
transformation and healing tends to minimize or ignore the
dimension of partnership with the Spirit of God as essential to the
very process of pastoral counseling.

As in all other arts and forms of ministry, the walk of
counseling assumes the gracious presence of God's Spirit, whose
participation is acknowledged and whose ultimate guidance
pastoral counselors are expected to seek and honor. To care in the
name and in the manner of Christ is to care in the power of the
Holy Spirit and in partnership with the Spirit. Interestingly,
according to John's Gospel (chapters 14–16) Jesus taught that the
Holy Spirit is the *parakletos*—comforter, advocate, helper, and
counselor—the one who, like Jesus, is a caring presence alongside
disciples as they journey through life. Further, John's version of
the commissioning—"As the Father has sent me, so I send you"
(20:21)—precedes empowering by the Spirit to participate in

---

[6] Consider also Donald Capps's discussion of these issues, in *Living Stories:
Pastoral Counseling in Congregational Context* (Minneapolis: Fortress Press, 1998),
207–21; and *Giving Counsel: A Minister's Guidebook* (Saint Louis: Chalice Press,
2001), 200–10. "We need to be wary of the view that it is the pastoral relationship
itself that heals," Capps writes. "We devalue the individual's own resources and
the many ways in which God's love manifests itself in human community and
the natural world when we give too much credit—or place too much blame—on
the pastoral relationship itself" (*Giving Counsel*, 205).

ministry (20:22–23). In this light, we may view pastoral counselors as specially called, authorized, and enabled ministering people. They become partners in the caring, sustaining, liberating, and healing work that is the business of the Spirit as they also walk alongside others, although the walk may sometimes be a brief one. Therefore, we must appreciate the pastoral counselor's relationship to counselees as expressing not only empathic engagement but incarnational presence as well.[7]

AS THEY FACE LIFE'S CHALLENGES AND STRUGGLES

Pastoral counseling was helpful for Karen and Raúl because it provided a good setting, an appropriate process, and valuable resources to help them think about their sense that something was not right and to do something about it. As they discussed their respective genograms, they remembered family anecdotes and stories, sometimes lightheartedly, and recognized significant patterns, events, and influences that had shaped the character of each of them. As they pondered the results of an instrument designed to identify styles of communication and ways of dealing with interpersonal conflict, they talked more clearly about difficulties they had faced in their relationship and began to visualize and to try out better alternatives. They began to understand more fully that marriage involves the convergence of two different unfolding stories that bring both complementarity and contradiction. They also began to comprehend their shared responsibility to weave together a new life tapestry. Further, their pastor helped them appreciate afresh their multiple gifts, as well as resources from the Christian tradition associated with the themes of love, grace, covenant, and blessing.

The new definition of pastoral counseling as a special form and setting of pastoral care in the ministry of the church began with *a distinctive way of walking with others*. It continues, *as they face life's challenges and struggles*. The choice of words is deliberate,

---

[7] For this notion of incarnational presence I am indebted to Marcus Smucker, "An Emerging Theology of Ministry: Incarnational Presence," in *Understanding Ministerial Leadership: Essays Contributing to a Developing Theology of Ministry*, ed. John A. Esau (Elkhart: Institute of Mennonite Studies, 1995), 100–13.

although somewhat arbitrary, because I attempt to avoid using terms and concepts directly connected with psychopathology and psychotherapy. I reiterate here that pastoral counselors must not view their task primarily in terms of mental health, emotional adjustment, personal growth, or similar psychological notions; neither should they understand, practice, or teach pastoral counseling as a subtype of clinical psychology or primarily as a branch of the psychotherapy industry.

In North America, pastoral counselors have often been considered one of the major groups of those who offer mental health care, together with psychiatrists, psychologists, and social workers. Let me be clear that I am *not* against pastoral counselors becoming specialized psychotherapists in the narrow sense of the term. Nevertheless, it is my conviction, first, that the practice of psychotherapy per se neither defines nor determines the practice and the theory of pastoral counseling; and second, that psychotherapy, strictly speaking, is not the pastoral counselor's first call or obligation. A related conviction and concern is that Christian psychologists, psychiatrists, and social workers must be challenged and educated to practice their professions consistently in a Christian manner, as I suggested in the previous chapter. Indeed, I am convinced that the more consistently Christian mental health care providers practice in a Christian manner, the less prominent becomes the need for pastoral psychotherapists as a distinct, certified profession.

Therefore, *as a special dimension of ministry and of pastoral care in particular, the primary concern pastoral counseling must address is helping people live wholesome and faithful lives in the midst of their normal human journey.* I thus propose to de-emphasize the therapeutic focus to the extent that such focus is viewed and enacted in a medical model, with preferential or even exclusive attention to malfunction, disability, or pathology. I certainly affirm the healing dimensions of pastoral counseling broadly understood (in addition to the guiding and nurturing, reconciling, supporting, and liberating dimensions of this ministry). Further, let us keep in mind that several expressions of pastoral care other than counseling—such as anointing and prayer, healing rituals, spiritual deliverance, and others—can also be powerfully healing. We should remember that the Greek *therapeia* means a helping, serving, healing relationship; a *therapon* (from which the word therapist derives) is one who helps, serves, and heals. Further, the Latin translation for *therapon* is *ministerium,* from which the word *minister* comes. Hence, the roots of therapy and ministry are closely intertwined. In this sense, the pastoral relationship has from its beginning been regarded literally as a kind of therapeutic relationship, reductionistic distortions notwithstanding!

The next two sections include brief descriptions of typical situations people encounter that may become the agenda for pastoral counseling. These are illustrations from my experience as counselor in various settings, from the supervision of my students, and from the reported practice of pastors and colleagues in the field. I follow these vignettes with a statement of practical guidelines or principles pertaining to specific dimensions and foci of pastoral counseling. I do not intend the categorization of occasions for pastoral counseling as challenges or struggles to be always clearly distinguishable; they are on a continuum. In any event, I assume that those seeking care for existential challenges will experience differing kinds and degrees of distress, depending on a variety of factors and circumstances.

EXISTENTIAL CHALLENGES

Joe is considering a change of jobs. He realizes, at forty-eight, that he needs to evaluate his unclear sense of vocation in light of his faith. Pastoral counseling offers an opportunity to examine other areas of Joe's life, beginning with his marriage and relationships with his children.

During the last few weeks, Ron has been feeling, in his words, very anxious and tense. He wants to find out whether he should consult a mental health professional. Ron's pastor helps him make an informed decision while reassuring him of the church's support.

Peter thinks he gets angry too often and has begun to wonder whether the problem is a matter of sin, weakness, or something else.

Irma is a single young adult with a successful career. She has begun to feel pressure—both external and internal—to try to establish a meaningful long-term relationship. Irma takes the opportunity to talk over her concerns with a female pastoral caregiver who has recently joined her church's pastoral staff to assist people in the church in dealing with issues of life and faith.

Dorothy and Mark have decided to get married. They love each other and know each other well (in fact, they have become sexually intimate) and feel they do not need to go through the premarital guidance program stipulated by the church.

Marie and Sam have tried to conceive a child for several years. They have serious questions about alternatives available; in addition to medical advice, they are looking for guidance about ethical and theological issues associated with those alternatives.

Evan and Brenda attended the church-sponsored marriage enrichment retreat. They want to work further to enrich their marriage as they approach their tenth anniversary.

José and Anita, a Hispanic couple, have serious questions about their culturally conditioned ways of relating and expressing affection among adults, and of practicing discipline at home. Are their ways better (or more Christian) than those they have found in the U.S.? Is it the other way around?

In light of a recent church-sponsored parent orientation emphasis, Greg and Tonya want to consult a pastoral counselor about the best ways to guide their children's behavior and to prevent and correct undesirable attitudes and actions. They are particularly interested in the issue of rewards and punishments.

Susan's mother is becoming increasingly incapacitated and has decided to stop taking medications except those to manage physical pain. Susan wants to talk over ethical issues that her mother raises, at times explicitly, about letting nature takes its course and about the right to die, for example.

Len and Olivia feel uneasy about the possibility of placing Len's father in a nursing home against his wishes, although this appears to them to be the best alternative available. Taking the initiative, their pastor offers to walk with Len and Olivia, to help them think through their concerns with sensitivity and integrity.

The category I identify as existential challenges includes what I call the ministries of discernment, orientation, and nurture. Pastoral counselors must function as Christian sages, or wise guides, especially, although not exclusively, in these instances. The content and the specific objectives of counseling those facing the challenges I have mentioned, and countless similar situations, clearly and explicitly relate to the need to make wise choices and to live and relate wisely. This is in accord with my proposal that wisdom in the light of God is, indeed, the heart of pastoral counseling. In connection with the need for guidance in wise decision making, I want to elaborate on two general principles that I introduced in the first chapter.

First, *pastoral counseling must recover its function and value as a ministry of discernment.* Life challenges all of us to practice good judgment, to choose well, and to make wise decisions in a wide variety of dimensions and situations, including diverse kinds of moral dilemmas, sexuality, vocational choices, professional quests, and so on. Much could be said about the need to exercise discernment, and the role of pastoral counselors in this regard, especially because of the inherent ethical and moral dimensions involved. William Willimon explains well that pastoral care involves not simply caring for others where they are, but working with them and with God so that they may move to a better location; the Christian faith links pastoral care to moral transformation.[8] Rebekah L. Miles presents the best argument in favor of reclaiming moral guidance as a crucial part of the ministry of pastoral care and counseling.[9] Obviously, the contribution of ethicists is necessary and welcome in this area.[10] Further, pastoral counselors should see discernment as a major task in pastoral

---

[8] William Willimon, *Pastor: The Theology and Practice of Ordained Ministry* (Louisville: Abingdon Press, 2002), chapter 7, "The Pastor As Counselor: Care That Is Christian."

[9] Rebekah L. Miles, *The Pastor As Moral Guide* (Minneapolis: Fortress Press, 1999).

[10] See, for instance, James M. Gustafson, "Moral Discernment in the Christian Life," in *Norm and Context in Christian Ethics* (New York: Scribners, 1968), ed. Gene Outka and Paul Ramsey, 17–36; and Gustafson, "The Minister As Moral Counselor," in *Journal of Psychology and Christianity* 3, no. 4 (1984): 16–22. For an excellent article by a pastoral theologian and counselor, see James N. Lapsley, "Moral Dilemmas in Pastoral Perspective," in *Dictionary of Pastoral Care and Counseling,* ed. Rodney J. Hunter (Nashville: Abingdon Press, 1990), 752–5. See Miles, *The Pastor As Moral Guide,* chapters 1 and 2.

counseling, in continuity with the expected, ongoing discerning process that constitutes the life of discipleship on a daily basis.[11]

Wise pastoral counselors help others recognize and deal with *limits*, that is, unchangeable facts (for example, one cannot undo unwise decisions and choices made in the past, and one cannot change the behavior of others). They also help others identify *limitations*, in the sense of conditions they may overcome or transform either by discovering untested alternatives or by mobilizing idle or untapped personal capabilities and potential. Thus, pastoral counselors also help people unveil and affirm certain gifts, dispositions, and available resources; identify the better of possible choices; and develop a sense of responsibility and accountability. They also assist people in deciding whether other specialized forms of assistance, such as legal, medical, spiritual, or psychological help, are needed. Then they assist people in finding the best attention and care available.

I do not assume that everyone will need pastoral counseling in order to make wise decisions. Rather, the primary role of pastoral counselors is to be available to assist people whenever their need to discern and to decide becomes an existential challenge, a situation they cannot or should not face alone or with the assistance of those who are normally around them. This responsibility stands in line with a noble pastoral tradition going back thousands of years.

Second, *a ministry of guidance and nurture must include a specific focus on marriage and family in the framework of the faith community.* As one example, pastoral counselors need to be available to assist people with premarital preparation. They can do so, for instance, by encouraging a couple to learn more about their respective families and their converging personal stories, and by assisting them to plan their wedding and to further visualize specific challenges and possibilities of their life together.[12] Pastoral

---

[11] Fittingly enough, discernment is one of the practices highlighted in Dorothy C. Bass, ed., *Practicing Our Faith: A Way of Life for a Searching People* (San Francisco: Jossey-Bass, 1997); see the essay by Frank Rogers Jr., "Discernment," 105–18.

[12] See Herbert Anderson and Robert Cotton Fite, *Becoming Married* (Louisville: Westminster John Knox Press, 1993); and Charles W. Taylor, *Premarital Guidance* (Minneapolis: Fortress Press, 1999).

counselors must also be capable of helping people discern when not to get married, and how to live wholesome lives as unmarried people.

The area of marriage enrichment is another priority for pastoral counseling. It includes a variety of possibilities, such as encouragement and guidance, resources and processes for improving communication and conflict resolution, understanding and consideration of family systems and dynamics, and special attention to such relational dimensions as sexuality and roles. In principle, I do not expect pastoral counselors to become family therapists in a specialized sense. However, understanding of and sensitivity to the dynamics of family systems and family life is essential for their pastoral work, not only with couples and families, but also with individuals. Pastoral counselors must also turn their attention to two specific areas: nurturing and enriching the multifaceted life of the family and its seasons, and especially, helping families and congregations become more wholesome, caring environments. This responsibility includes the development and guidance of children and youth, communication and conflict resolution, and prevention of as well as timely and adequate response to crises, in the context of faith and the larger community.

EXISTENTIAL STRUGGLES

Wes and Margaret have learned that their unborn child is certain to have a serious abnormality; one of the specialists has recommended abortion as a sensible decision for the benefit of everybody included.

Pat's pastor suspects that the treatment Pat has been receiving from her husband amounts to emotional and verbal abuse, and perhaps physical abuse as well.

Emily and Fred have been divorced for two years; Emily, a church member, seeks to improve their troubled communication primarily for the sake of their children.

Kate, a single mother, seeks help in the face of difficulties relating to her rebellious adolescent son. She is concerned that he is in bad company most of the time and may be involved with drugs.

Diane's husband has been engaged in an adulterous relationship. Diane needs to deal not only with her own sense of betrayal but also with such key questions as: what are the facts, who should know about the situation, and what should she do about it?

Former friends Sarah and Carol experience deep hurts and have not been able to understand and forgive each other; they are finally ready for mediation (or one of them is ready to take the first step).

The pastor takes the initiative to approach Wayne about an unacknowledged offense on Wayne's part.

Nate has come out as gay. His parents and one of his siblings are deeply distressed. The pastor wants to offer support to the whole family.

Sonia and Frank have just learned that their child is gravely ill.

Brad has experienced the sudden loss of a dear friend in an automobile accident.

Dan confronts the feared diagnosis of a terminal illness when his doctors confirm that he is suffering from an aggressive kind of cancer.

After surgery, Rachel realizes that she will never be her family's strong support again. She must deal with many losses and is searching for a new sense of divine grace.

John has worked for a company for sixteen years. Now he faces the impending loss of his job because of downsizing, and he is devastated.

Nancy and her three children have been left alone in the U.S. after her husband was summarily detained as an illegal alien and deported to Central America.

Caring for people facing existential struggles entails the ministries of reconciling, supporting, and healing. Included in the category of existential struggles are the deeply troubling situations that are most likely to demand the specialized services of mental health professionals; however, by no means all people confronting situations I recognize as existential struggles will need such services. I will suggest two additional practical guidelines that pertain to the role of pastoral counselors who are ministering to those engaged in these life struggles. Before I present these guidelines, however, I insert a parenthetical consideration about the interaction between pastoral counseling and mental health.

As I have noted, situations that I identify as existential struggles include the dimensions of deep trouble, conflict, trauma, and pain. Nevertheless, pastoral counselors should not understand existential struggles a priori or primarily in terms of mental health and psychopathology and as therefore requiring therapeutic intervention. In other words, one should not assume that these situations, by definition, must be considered from a psychiatric perspective and treated using a psychiatric approach. Clearly, under some circumstances that I identify here as existential struggles, a person, a couple, or a family may well need therapeutic assistance by a mental health professional. Pastoral counselors must be equipped to discern such an instance accurately and in a timely manner. Furthermore, pastoral counselors need to be well acquainted with mental health and other care resources available in the larger community; they need to know when and how to refer, and how to collaborate with other professional caregivers. Along the same lines, pastoral counselors must recognize that whatever we do in pastoral counseling also affects mental health and emotional adjustment, however defined.[13] This is true regardless of whether the presenting concerns relate to growth, nurture, and prevention (existential challenges) or to reconciling, supporting, and healing (existential struggles).

When walking with those who are facing existential struggles, pastoral counselors must retain their roles as caregiving sages while also serving as mediators and reconcilers; they are covenant makers who are also healers.[14] I return now to practical

---

[13] Analogously, the content and forms of preaching, teaching, youth ministry, and other church ministries also influence people's mental health and emotional adjustment in diverse ways and degrees.

[14] Traditionally, the different dimensions and expressions of pastoral care have been understood in terms of guiding, sustaining, reconciling, and healing. See, for instance, William A. Clebsch and Charles R. Jakle, *Pastoral Care in Historical Perspective* (New York: Jason Aronson, 1975). These authors provide a discussion of those functions in the context of different historical periods. Other helpful sources on this topic include John T. McNeill, *A History of the Cure of Souls* (New

guidelines that speak to these aspects of the pastoral counselor's engagement with those wrestling with existential struggles. Taking the following two guidelines together with the two I presented earlier under the heading *existential challenges* (those pertaining to the discernment and guidance aspects of a pastoral counseling ministry), one finds a succinct picture of the fourfold responsibility of pastoral counseling as a ministry of the church.

The third element of this fourfold responsibility is reconciliation. *Pastoral counselors must engage in reconciliation ministry in a wide variety of situations.* Since forgiveness is one of the keys to wholeness and wise living—and the wise life is the reconciled life, in communion with God and neighbor—helping people forgive well and accept forgiveness is one of the major responsibilities of pastoral counselors.[15] Pastoral counselors must know how to function as mediators and agents of conflict transformation. Specifically, they need to know how to confront and to encourage awareness of offense and wrongdoing. They must encourage truthful confession and authentic repentance, as well as expression of pain and anger in the face of offense. Further, pastoral counselors must be able to guide the often laborious processes of forgiving and self-forgiving, of asking and receiving forgiveness, of healing memories, and of hopeful reconstruction of personal stories and family and communal futures, even in the face of nonrepairable hurt and persistent woundedness.[16] In sum, therefore, when considering healing in

York: Harper & Row, 1951); and Brooks E. Holifield, *A History of Pastoral Care in America: From Salvation to Self-Realization* (Nashville: Abingdon Press, 1983). For a more recent overview of pastoral care in the twentieth century and a sense of new directions in the field, see Charles V. Gerkin, *Introduction to Pastoral Care* (Nashville: Abingdon Press, 1997), especially chapters 2 and 3.

[15] On this topic, see David W. Augsburger, *Helping People Forgive* (Louisville: Westminster John Knox Press, 1996). Growing out of his conviction that human beings belong in community, Augsburger calls and makes the case for a new paradigm of forgiveness in which love, justice, reconciliation, and reconstruction are involved.

[16] One of the theoretical and practical challenges we face—especially when we understand peace and justice as foundational concepts for pastoral and practical theology—is to consider further continuities between various reconciliation ministries. An example is the apparent commonality observable between reconciliation ministries aimed at marriage, family, and interpersonal conflict

pastoral counseling settings, the first concern is the healing of broken relationships. In sum, pastoral counseling provides a unique setting for counselors to participate in the reconciliation ministry that God has entrusted to the Christian faith community (2 Cor. 5:18).

The ministry of healing is a fourth and final element needed in the pastoral counselor's role. *Pastoral counselors have a unique role to play in the face of the natural vulnerabilities of human life where healing is needed.* These include difficult transitions, developmental and accidental crises, sickness and trauma, loss and death. Some of these vulnerabilities relate directly to people's unwise choices, whether because of ignorance, negligence, or sin; they may also be the direct or indirect result of the unwise choices and hurtful behaviors of others, again with greater or lesser degree of moral responsibility. Whatever the specific circumstances, pastoral counselors must help people see reality clearly, trust God deeply, and restore their lives hopefully. They may do this by participating in various forms of supportive and healing ministry. A pastoral counselor may help another grieve, lament, activate available resources, face impending death (one's own or the death of a loved one, whether more or less timely), assume due responsibility, be freed from undue burdens of guilt, find consolation and meaning, recover a sense of hope, and so on. Pastoral counselors thus provide support and guidance in the midst of suffering, even when those seeking care are also receiving assistance elsewhere.

I add a special word here about those individuals and families in special need whom society often neglects or overlooks, those who are poor, unschooled, aliens, immigrants, mentally ill, and imprisoned. *Pastoral counselors must recover the noble tradition of pastoral care and counseling as a form of Christian service especially available to marginalized, victimized, poor, and oppressed people.*[17] In fact, when pastoral counselors make pastoral care and counseling available to people in these circumstances, the narrow confines of the field and the limitations of the prevailing models become even

---

situations and those ministries working for mediation or peace and justice between groups.

[17] Cf. Gerkin, *An Introduction to Pastoral Care,* 89–90.

more apparent.[18] Fortunately, during the last few years the theoretical and practical horizons of pastoral care and counseling have expanded, thanks to contributions that more explicitly and consistently address the socioeconomic and political dimensions that condition our lives.[19]

THAT THEY MAY LIVE WISELY
IN THE LIGHT OF GOD

Karen and Raúl anticipated along with their pastor that counseling would help them acknowledge anew the rich and unique features of their individual life stories and faith journeys. They met that goal by focusing on ways each of them had experienced family and other relationships and had developed a philosophy of life and sense of vocation. They addressed questions of identity and sense of direction, assuming the perspective of a primary identity as a woman or man of God. Karen and Raúl had also agreed on another goal: pastoral counseling would help them start visualizing, with realism, hope, and anticipated joy, new ways in which their relationship could further mature. That happened as transformative learning took place not only in the emotional, relational, and social dimensions of their lives, but also in moral and spiritual dimensions.

---

[18] My involvement as a pastoral counselor volunteer at a community health care center (see chapter 3, footnote 2) and a caregiver in my local congregation has helped me better understand both the limitations of prevailing practices and the potential for a reenvisioned model of pastoral counseling as a ministry of the church.

[19] For valuable references, see chapter 3, footnote 37. In addition consider G. Michael Cordner, ed., *Pastoral Theology's and Pastoral Psychology's Contributions to Helping Heal a Violent World* (Sukarta, Indonesia: International Pastoral Care Network for Social Responsibility and DÁBARA, 1996); James Newton Poling, *The Abuse of Power: A Theological Problem* (Nashville: Abingdon Press, 1991); and *Deliver Us From Evil: Resisting Racial and Gender Oppression* (Minneapolis: Fortress Press, 1996); Emmanuel Y. Lartey, *In Living Color: An Intercultural Approach to Pastoral Care and Counseling*, 2d ed. (London and New York: Jessica Kingsley Publications, 2003); Stephen Pattison, *Pastoral Care and Liberation Theology* (Cambridge: Cambridge University Press, 1994); Pamela D. Couture, *Blessed Are the Poor? Women's Poverty, Family Policy, and Practical Theology* (Louisville: Abingdon Press, 1991); and *Seeing Children, Seeing God: A Practical Theology of Children and Poverty* (Nashville: Abingdon Press, 2000).

In the final counseling session, Karen and Raúl agreed to schedule three appointments for pre-wedding guidance. Their pastor gave them the names of other couples with strong marriages who would be willing to share from their experiences, in the manner of mentors. They were encouraged to choose one of those couples to meet with them from time to time. The pastor would make the initial arrangements. Thus, the church, as a community of care and wisdom, was continuing to respond to Karen and Raúl.

It seems that human cultures, as far as we can historically ascertain, have always included competing wisdoms and alternative views of humanization or human becoming. Our own time provides many illustrations of this point, especially given the prominent place of psychology (including modern psychological systems and approaches)[20] as a special kind of wisdom. Indeed, for some time now, psychology has played a major role in the dominant western culture by the lure and pervasive power of its concepts and technologies.[21] Psychology functions as wisdom not

---

[20] Research has demonstrated that the religious beliefs of counselors and psychologists correlate with their clinical orientations. For a recent study, see Dyer P. Bilgrave and Robert H. Deluty, "Religious Beliefs and Therapeutic Orientations of Clinical and Counseling Psychologists," *Journal for the Scientific Study of Religion* 37 (June 1998): 329–49. These researchers found that psychologists who affirmed orthodox Christian beliefs tended to endorse the cognitive-behavioral orientation, whereas those who affirmed eastern and mystical beliefs tended to endorse humanistic and existential orientations. Bilgrave and Deluty ask whether the tension typically elicited by either psychoanalytic or humanistic ideology is less problematic than the tension raised by the deep assumptions of the cognitive-behavioral perspective.

[21] Woolfolk discusses this topic of the dominant role of psychology/ psychotherapy in our culture from a philosophical perspective in *The Cure of Souls*; see especially the introduction and chapters 1–4. Other valuable recent treatments of this topic are Philip Rieff, *The Triumph of the Therapeutic* (New York: Harper & Row, 1966); Christopher Lasch, *The Culture of Narcissism: American Life in an Age of Diminished Expectations* (New York: Norton, 1979); Alasdair C. MacIntyre, *After Virtue: A Study in Moral Theory*, 2d ed. (Notre Dame: University of Notre Dame Press, 1984); Robert Bellah, et al., *Habits of the Heart: Individualism and Commitment in American Life* (New York: Harper & Row, 1985); and Charles J. Sykes, *A Nation of Victims: The Decay of American Character* (New York: St. Martin's Press, 1992).

only by defining wellness, health, maturity, and illness, but also by becoming a principal source of personal identity and vocation. It has become the key to self-understanding as well as the main guide for ordering our lives. Don Browning discusses this situation from a theological perspective. He points out the ethical and metaphysical horizon of some of the major contemporary psychotherapeutic psychologies by analyzing their implicit principles of obligation and the metaphors deeply embedded in and around their conceptual systems. Browning's critique of these dimensions of modern psychologies draws specifically on resources of Jewish and Christian religious traditions.[22]

Psychological language and imagery have become prevalent in many areas of the church's thought and work. As a result, they frequently trivialize and subvert (i.e., psychologize) the goals of ministry, and convert them into socialized versions of personal enrichment, growth, or fulfillment. Whenever that happens, we focus on personal needs as defined primarily by psychological categories, embellished with religious language, and conditioned by marketing concerns. Further, we can recognize two related temptations confronted by both church members and pastoral leaders: first, the attractiveness of psychological sources for metaphors of human wholeness and becoming, understandings about how to achieve wholeness, and direction in doing so; and second, the seductiveness of psychological images and notions of what faith and growth in Christian life mean and involve.[23]

---

[22] Don S. Browning, *Religious Thought and the Modern Psychologies: A Critical Conversation in the Theology of Culture* (Philadelphia: Fortress Press, 1987). For a critical, theologically informed evangelical evaluation and appropriation of contemporary psychotherapies, see Stanton L. Jones and Richard E. Butman, *Modern Psychotherapies: A Comprehensive Christian Appraisal* (Downers Grove: InterVarsity Press, 1991). Paul C. Vitz offers a trenchant critical analysis of modern psychology in *Psychology As Religion: The Cult of Self-Worship*, 2d ed. (Grand Rapids: Eerdmans, 1994).

[23] For a study from a sociological perspective, see Marsha G. Witten, *All Is Forgiven: The Secular Message in American Protestantism* (Princeton: Princeton University Press, 1993). Witten conducted an in-depth analysis of preaching based on Luke 15; sermons on the prodigal son which she analyzed came from pulpits of the Presbyterian Church (USA) and the Southern Baptist Convention. She found that the image of God had the softened demeanor of an understanding

Our understanding of wisdom in the light of God encourages us to come to terms with psychology as a powerful form of conventional and pragmatic wisdom in our culture. We find a colorful textbook illustration of the role of psychology as conventional wisdom in our culture in Charles Spencer's tribute to his sister Diana, the late Princess of Wales. In that solemn funeral moment at Westminster Abbey, he said at the core of an eloquent speech: "Diana explained to me once that it was her innermost feelings of suffering that made it possible for her to connect with her constituency of the rejected. And here we come to another truth about her. For all the status, the glamour, the applause, Diana remained throughout a very insecure person at heart, almost childlike in her desire to do good for others so she could release herself from deep feelings of unworthiness of which her eating disorders were merely a symptom. The world sensed this part of her character and cherished her for her vulnerability whilst admiring her for her honesty."[24] What I want to underscore here is that both Spencer's reference to Diana's self-analysis and his own perspective and appraisal—he confidently calls it a truth about her—are unequivocally psychological interpretations (psychoanalytical, actually). The speech includes no ethical/moral or faith/spiritual considerations. Further, the crowd's response at the end of the speech appeared to confirm that Spencer had spoken truth. This remarkable episode, witnessed by millions of people around the globe, is a clear example of a feature that characterizes our dominant western culture: psychology's determinative role in shaping people's sense of identity and vocation, and their search for wholeness. This includes what some call the triumph of the therapeutic or the medicalization of character. Sadly, we heard much about Diana Spencer's search for healing through subjecting herself to an incredible variety of therapies, both conventional and unconventional. Yet we heard nothing about her faith and whether she also sought spiritual healing in the deep wellsprings of the Christian faith. One might have hoped for more; after all, as

---

and loving daddy with the primary function of providing psychological comfort to individual church members.

[24] *People*, 22 September 1997, 70.

princess of Wales she was also the mother of the future head of the Church of England.

Pastoral counselors need to identify, test, and challenge the metaphysical and ethical dimensions of psychology as a practical human science. These dimensions are, of course, inherently metapsychological; their source is not psychology as such, but some other ideology. We must keep in mind that psychology offers a variety of definitions for health, maturity, emotional adjustment, functionality, and growth. These varying definitions point to differing understandings of human becoming, because they grow out of diverse sources.[25] I reiterate therefore that pastoral counselors must articulate the overall purpose and specific goals of pastoral counseling in terms of our discernment and understanding of God's wisdom, rather than in terms of the conventional and pragmatic wisdom of psychology and psychotherapy in the dominant western culture.

The contributions of psychology and psychotherapy are nevertheless essential for the pastoral counselor, in terms of both content (for instance, understandings of family systems and psychopathology) and process (for example, guidelines concerning the counseling relationship and communication dynamics).[26] Alternatives for construing the relationship of psychological and theological perspectives have been explored; the options involve epistemological and methodological issues.[27] Among evangelical Christian psychologists there has been a lively discussion over the last thirty

---

[25] This recognizing, testing, and challenging is precisely what Browning does in the case of six of the most influential psychologies, beginning with Freudian psychoanalysis. He also demonstrates how to do it with intellectual honesty and theological integrity.

[26] Two resources are Brad W. Johnson and William L. Johnson, *The Pastor's Guide to Psychological Disorders and Treatments* (New York: Haworth Pastoral Press, 2000); and William R. Miller and Kathleen A. Jackson, *A Practical Psychology for Pastors*, 2d ed., (Englewood Cliffs, N.J.: Prentice Hall, 1995).

[27] For a brief review of possible Christian responses to secular psychology as it informs pastoral counseling, see R. F. Hurding, "Pastoral Care, Counseling and Psychotherapy," in *New Dictionary of Christian Ethics and Pastoral Theology*, ed. David J. Atkinson and David H. Field (Downers Grove: InterVarsity Press, 1995), 78–85. Hurding describes the five main options as assimilative, excluding, pragmatic eclectic, perspectivalist, and integrational.

years about the relationship between psychology and Christian faith, sparked especially by the possibility of integrating psychological and theological perspectives and contributions.[28] On this point, I agree with Deborah van Deusen Hunsinger that the key to a fitting appropriation of psychological perspectives by pastoral counselors lies in the following three methodological conditions.[29] First, we must respect the integrity of psychology as a human science in providing a distinct reading of the human situation, with the understanding that other readings, including that of theology, are possible and indeed necessary. Second, diverse readings must be kept side by side in our search for complementary insights and a more complete knowledge. Finally, pastoral counselors must hold these disciplines in an asymmetrical relationship, maintaining the conceptual priority of theology over psychology. In other words, the contributions of psychology and psychotherapy must be subordinate to claims, frameworks, and perspectives grounded in the biblical and theological foundations of pastoral care and counseling. Simply said, those other indispensable contributions must be seen, critically appropriated, and used according to standards and

---

[28] For a recent review of discussion on integration, and new perspectives and analyses, see *Journal of Psychology and Christianity* 15 (summer 1996), entire issue. In addition to material typically included in *Journal of Psychology and Theology*, several pertinent contributions define the contours of Christian psychology and are particularly helpful for pastoral counseling practice and theory. They include C. Stephen Evans, *Wisdom and Humanness in Psychology: Prospects for a Christian Approach* (Grand Rapids: Baker Books, 1989); Jones and Butman, *Modern Psychotherapies*, chapters 1, 15, 16; Robert C. Roberts and Mark R. Talbot, eds., *Limning the Psyche: Explorations in Christian Psychology* (Grand Rapids: Eerdmans, 1997); and Mark R. McMinn and Timothy R. Phillips, eds., *Care for the Soul: Exploring the Intersection of Psychology and Theology* (Downers Grove: InterVarsity Press, 2001).

[29] The three conditions point to the so-called Chalcedonian pattern as applied to the epistemological and methodological questions of relating psychology to theology. For a systematic study of the pattern and its applicability in pastoral counseling, see Deborah van Deusen Hunsinger, *Theology and Pastoral Counseling: A New Interdisciplinary Approach* (Grand Rapids: Eerdmans, 1995), especially chapter 3. See also, by the same author, "An Interdisciplinary Map for Christian Counselors: Theology and Psychology in Pastoral Counseling," in *Care for the Soul*, ed. McMinn and Phillips, 218–40.

values of wholeness and abundant life, which God graciously reveals to us as real and authentic wisdom, wisdom in the light of God.

CONCLUSION

Throughout this book, I have maintained that pastoral counseling is a distinctive way of walking with others, so that they may become wiser in the light of God. By way of conclusion, I offer a summary of the differences this wisdom perspective might make for the pastoral counseling field, and specifically for the role of the pastoral counselor. My pastoral counseling research, grounded in practice, documents the results of applying a practical theological perspective to the study of this important form of care ministry. Through my work I have sought to provide a constructive response to the particular critique of pastoral counseling that I described in the introduction. In sum, then, what do we gain by viewing, engaging in, and teaching pastoral counseling in terms of wisdom?

First, adopting wisdom in the light of God as the ground metaphor rebuilds the theoretical framework and theological foundations of pastoral care on a solid footing. With these in place, we may freshly appreciate the distinctive potential of pastoral counselors as *practical theologians*. Further, we may understand pastoral counseling itself as a practice of wisdom and a way of doing practical theology that gives attention to the empirical, hermeneutical, and strategic dimensions and goals of that task.

Second, the paradigm I have presented in this book sheds light, both practically and theoretically, on a fundamental issue: the integration of psychological and theological perspectives. The metaphor of wisdom in the light of God supplies a worthy principle for guiding, understanding, and carrying out a type of pastoral counseling that is both fully counseling and fully pastoral. Further, the metaphor illuminates the correspondence between process and goals in Christian ministry, and calls for pastoral counselors to reaffirm their work as *pastoral theologians*.

Third, and closely related to the previous points, when wisdom in the light of God (rather than mental health or some alternative metaphor) defines the nature and orientation of the form of Christian ministry, we may readily recognize the ethical dimensions and the moral context of pastoral counseling. Therefore, the special responsibilities of pastoral counselors as *ethicists and moral guides* also become more clearly apparent.

Finally, although pastoral counseling belongs within the so-called private ministry domain, directly engaging only two or a few people at any one time, it can involve prophetic and transformative dimensions that confront the conventional and pragmatic wisdom of our time. Indeed, beyond the inherent limitations of the settings and processes normally involved, pastoral counseling can and should serve the transformation of culture. Hence, wisdom in the light of God orients pastoral counselors to walk with others in hope toward a society of freedom, justice, peace, love, and wholeness, and uniquely calls them to become *therapists for a better world*.

Selected bibliography

Anderson, Ray S. *Christians Who Counsel: The Vocation of Wholistic Therapy.* Grand Rapids: Zondervan Publishing House, 1990.

Augsburger, David. *Pastoral Counseling Across Cultures.* Philadelphia: Westminster Press, 1986.

Brown, Warren S. *Understanding Wisdom: Sources, Science and Society.* Philadelphia and London: Templeton Foundation Press, 2000.

Browning, Don S. *Religious Ethics and Pastoral Care.* Philadelphia: Fortress Press, 1983.

———. *Religious Thought and the Modern Psychologies: A Critical Conversation in the Theology of Culture.* Philadelphia: Fortress Press, 1987.

Capps, Donald. *Living Stories: Pastoral Counseling in Congregational Context.* Minneapolis: Fortress Press, 1998.

———. *Giving Counsel: A Minister's Guidebook.* St. Louis: Chalice Press, 2001.

———. *Reframing: A New Method in Pastoral Care.* Minneapolis, Fortress Press, 1990.

Childs, Brian H. *Short-Term Pastoral Counseling.* Rev. ed. New York: Haworth Pastoral Press, 2000.

Clinebell, Howard. *Basic Types of Pastoral Care and Counseling: Resources for the Ministry of Healing and Growth.* Nashville: Abingdon Press, 1984.

Culbertson, Philip. *Caring for God's People: Counseling and Christian Wholeness.* Minneapolis: Fortress Press, 2000.

Couture, Pamela D. *Seeing Children, Seeing God: A Practical Theology of Children and Poverty.* Nashville: Abingdon Press, 2000.

———, and Rodney. J. Hunter, eds. *Pastoral Care and Social Conflict.* Nashville: Abingdon Press, 1995.

Dayringer, Richard. *The Heart of Pastoral Counseling: Healing through Relationships*. Rev. ed. New York: Haworth Pastoral Press, 1998.

DeMarinis, Valerie M. *Critical Caring: A Feminist Model for Pastoral Psychology*. Louisville: Westminster John Knox Press, 1993.

Dittes, James E. *Pastoral Counseling: The Basics*. Louisville: Westminster John Knox Press, 1999.

Dueck, Alvin C. *Between Jerusalem and Athens: Ethical Perspectives on Culture, Religion and Psychotherapy*. Grand Rapids: Baker Books, 1995.

Fowler, James W. *Becoming Adult, Becoming Christian: Adult Development and Christian Faith*. Rev. ed. San Francisco: Jossey-Bass Publishers, 2000.

———. *Faithful Change: The Personal and Public Challenges of Post-Modern Life*. Nashville: Abingdon Press, 1996.

Gerkin, Charles V. *An Introduction to Pastoral Care*. Nashville: Abingdon Press, 1997.

———. *The Living Human Document: Re-visioning Pastoral Counseling in a Hermeneutical Mode*. Nashville: Abingdon Press, 1984.

———. *Prophetic Pastoral Care: A Christian Vision of Life Together*. Nashville: Abingdon Press, 1991.

Gorsuch, Nancy J. *Introducing Feminist Pastoral Care and Counseling*. Cleveland: Pilgrim Press, 2001.

Graham, Elaine. *Transforming Practice: Pastoral Theology in an Age of Uncertainty*. London: Mowbray, 1996.

Graham, Larry Kent. *Care of Persons, Care of Worlds: A Psychosystems Approach to Pastoral Care and Counseling*. Nashville: Abingdon Press, 1992.

Heitink, Gerben. *Practical Theology: History, Theory, Action Domains*. Trans. Reinder Bruinsma. Grand Rapids: Eerdmans, 1999.

Howe, Leroy T. *The Image of God: A Theology for Pastoral Care and Counseling*. Nashville: Abingdon Press, 1995.

Hunsinger, Deborah van Deusen. *Theology and Pastoral Counseling: A New Interdisciplinary Approach.* Grand Rapids: Eerdmans, 1995.

Johnson, W. Brad, and William L. Johnson. *The Pastor's Guide to Psychological Disorders and Treatments.* New York: Haworth Pastoral Press, 2000.

Lamothe, Ryan. *Revitalizing Faith through Pastoral Counseling.* Nashville: Abingdon Press, 2001.

Lartey, Emmanuel Y. *In Living Color: An Intercultural Approach to Pastoral Care and Counseling,* Rev. ed. London and New York: Jessica Kingsley Publications, 2003.

Loder, James E. *The Logic of the Spirit: Human Development in Theological Perspective.* San Francisco: Jossey-Bass Publishers, 1998.

———. *The Transforming Moment.* 2d ed. Colorado Springs: Helmers & Howard, 1989.

Louw, Daniël J. *A Mature Faith: Spiritual Direction and Anthropology in a Theology of Pastoral Care and Counseling.* Louvain: Peeters Press, 1999.

———. *A Pastoral Hermeneutics of Care and Encounter: A Theological Design for a Basic Theory, Anthropology, Method and Therapy.* Cape Town: Lux Verbi, 1999.

Lyall, David. *Counselling in the Spiritual and Pastoral Context.* Buckingham: Open University Press, 1995.

———. *Integrity of Pastoral Care.* London: SPCK, 2001.

Miles, Rebekah L. *The Pastor As Moral Guide.* Minneapolis: Fortress Press, 1999.

Miller, William R., and Kathleen A. Jackson. *Practical Psychology for Pastors.* 2d ed. Englewood Cliffs: Prentice Hall, 1995.

Miller-McLemore, Bonnie. *Also a Mother: Work and Family As Theological Dilemma.* Nashville: Abingdon Press, 1994.

Miller-McLemore, Bonnie J., and Brita L. Gill-Austern, eds. *Feminist and Womanist Pastoral Theology.* Nashville: Abingdon Press, 1999.

Moessner, Jeanne Stevenson, ed. *Through the Eyes of Women: Insights for Pastoral Care.* Minneapolis: Fortress Press, 1996.

Neuger, Christie Cozad. *Counseling Women: A Narrative, Pastoral Approach*. Minneapolis: Fortress Press, 2001.

Oden, Thomas C. *Pastoral Counsel*. Classical Pastoral Care Series, vol. 3. Grand Rapids: Baker Books, 1989.

Patton, John. *Pastoral Care in Context: An Introduction to Pastoral Care*. Louisville: Westminster John Knox Press, 1993.

———. *Pastoral Counseling: A Ministry of the Church*. Nashville: Abingdon Press, 1983.

Poling, James Newton. *The Abuse of Power: A Theological Problem*. Nashville: Abingdon Press, 1991.

———. *Deliver Us from Evil: Resisting Racial and Gender Oppression*. Minneapolis: Fortress Press, 1996.

———. *Render unto God: Economic Vulnerability, Family Violence, and Pastoral Theology*. St. Louis: Chalice Press, 2002.

Ramsay, Nancy J. *Pastoral Diagnosis: A Resource for Ministers of Care and Counseling*. Minneapolis: Fortress Press, 1998.

Stairs, Jean. *Listening for the Soul: Pastoral Care and Spiritual Direction*. Minneapolis: Fortress Press, 2000.

Stone, Howard H. *Brief Pastoral Counseling: Short-Term Approaches and Strategies*. Minneapolis: Fortress Press, 1994.

———. *Theological Context for Pastoral Caregiving: Word in Deed*. New York: Haworth Pastoral Press, 1996.

———, ed. *Strategies for Brief Pastoral Counseling*. Minneapolis: Fortress Press, 2001.

Vining, John Kie, *Spirit-Centered Counseling*. East Rockaway, N.Y.: Cummings & Hathaway, 1995.

Wicks, Robert J., and Barry K. Estadt, eds. *Pastoral Counseling in a Global Church: Voices from the Field*. Maryknoll: Orbis Books, 1993.

Wimberly, Edward P. *African American Pastoral Care*. Nashville: Abingdon Press, 1991.